SARC

DICTIONARY

A Lexicon of Cutting Remarks*

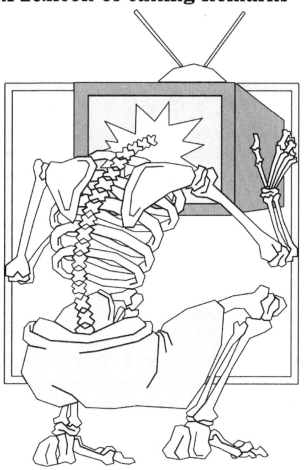

* Recommended only for those who possess the
incredibly rare ability to appreciate sharp humor

Welcome!

Let this sarcasm dictionary devour your soul. Brace yourself for a journey into the depths of snark-land, where every page will undoubtedly change your life...or not.

ACKNOWLEDGEMENTS

In the world of sarcasm, where words skillfully balance on the brink of meaning, gratitude takes an ironic twist.

I'd love to start by thanking the sleepless nights that made sure to chase me and haunt me during this journey. Your presence, much like an uninvited guest, provided encouragement and motivation, and for that, I am genuinely grateful.

Next, a big, warm thanks to coffee, my constant partner like super glue, for providing the energy and clarity needed to bring this project to life. Your ability to transform me from a non-functional human into a semi-alert writer has been a true marvel. Without your stimulating presence, this book might have ended up as confusing as a kid's drawing or a politician's speech.

Lastly, I must write down my appreciation to my ironic partner in sarcasm (crime), your humor infused life into these pages. Your ability to inject humor into even the most mundane or boring conversations has been invaluable.

To the sleepless nights, bottomless cups of coffee, and my ever-sarcastic life partner, I raise a figurative cup of espresso in your honor. Your contributions to this sarcastic book are immeasurable, and for that, I am genuinely, sincerely, and without a trace of sarcasm, grateful.

TABLE OF CONTENTS

PREFACE

WELCOME to a world where comedy is as smooth-flowing as a well-brewed cup of coffee and words are as sharp as knives. In the pages that follow we will explore the language of sarcasm and its subtle artistry.

SARCASM is a form of verbal irony where words do the cha-cha with their meanings, often used to express criticism, ridicule, or contempt. It involves the use of words to suggest exactly the opposite, often humorously or critically. For example, like saying, "My, you're up early!" to your buddy that woke up in the afternoon.

The term sarcasm is derived from the Greek word *"sarkasmos"*, which loosely translates to "tearing flesh" or "a cutting remark." Its first known use was in 1550. Today, it can also be found in everyday conversation and on social media platforms, resulting in laughters, eye rolls and... of course, the occasional facepalm.

Whether you've recently entered the land of sarcasm or think of yourself as a seasoned veteran, this dictionary serves as your trustworthy guide through the complex landscape of mischievous language.

KEEP IN MIND that sarcasm, is a unique form of humor, but it should always be delivered with empathy in mind. While sarcasm can make a conversation more engaging or lighten the mood, it can also cause misunderstanding or hurt feelings if not used appropriately.

So, dear reader, let's add a touch of playfulness to your conversations, where sarcasm rules supreme. Let the adventure begin, and may your sarcasm detector always be finely tuned!

The letter "A"

A is like an overachieving acrobat in the alphabet circus, always eager to leap to the front of the word and flaunt its angular antics. It's the attention-seeking diva, the apex predator of vowels, making other letters envy its audacity and angular allure. **A** for arrogance, indeed!

ABBREVIATION

A lazy way to write words by using fewer letters and making language look like it's on a diet, only to make the other person more confuse and spend more time into describing what you actually wanted to say.

ABDUCTION

The polite term for when aliens "borrow" you for a cosmic joyride and return you with no memory. Don't worry, they still prefer to go for cows in a field in the middle of nowhere.

ABOMINABLE

Something described as so utterly detestable that even a garbage can would refuse to associate with it.

ABSTINENCE

The act of voluntarily avoiding fun, pleasure, and all things enjoyable. See also: **DIETING.**

ABSURD

The feeling you get when you realize people are willing to spend hours watching cats play piano on the internet.

ACCIDENT

The universe's way of saying, "Surprise! Life is unpredictable, and so are potholes."

ACNE

A skin condition that strikes with impeccable timing, ensuring you have a massive pimple on your face just in time for every important event.

ACORNS

The tiny, nutty missiles that make squirrels appear both industrious and slightly deranged.

ACTOR

A master of disguise who pretends to be other people for a living, all while you struggle to be yourself.

ADDICTION

A passionate love affair with something that refuses to love you back, whether it's caffeine, social media, or hot sauce.

ADOPTION

The process of choosing a child and providing them with a loving home, unless you're talking about adopting a "rescue" plant, which usually ends in plant funerals.

ADVENTURE

An exciting journey filled with danger, excitement, and the constant fear that you forgot to pack enough snacks.

ADVERTISEMENT

A persuasive message designed to make you want something you never knew you needed, like pet insurance for your imaginary llama.

AESTHETIC

The term used by hipsters to describe things they like, which are often just old things with new price tags.

AFRO

A hairstyle that defies gravity, making you wonder if its wearer is secretly hiding snacks up there.

AGONY

The feeling that accompanies stepping on a LEGO brick, stubbing your toe, or watching your phone slip from your hand in slow motion.

AGRICULTURE

The art of convincing plants to grow in straight rows and resist the urge to take over the world.

AHCHOO

The involuntary announcement that your immune system has declared war on allergens.

AIMBOT

A video game cheat that magically turns your terrible aiming skills into a digital sharpshooter, while your opponents look on in disbelief.

AIMLESS

The feeling you get when you're wandering around the grocery store with no shopping list, hoping that inspiration will strike in the chip aisle.

AIRPLANE

A metal tube that defies the laws of gravity, while simultaneously testing your tolerance for small seats and subpar in-flight meals.

AIRPORT

A magical realm where you stand in lines longer than your actual flight and pay $10 for a lukewarm sandwich.

ALCOHOL

The solution to, and cause of, all of life's problems.

ALIEN

The cosmic tourist who still prefer to visit remote farms in the middle of nowhere, puzzled by our questionable choices like pineapple on pizzas .

ALLERGY

A special talent for turning harmless substances you didn't know existed, into your body's sworn enemies.

ALLIGATOR

A reptile that dresses like a dinosaur but lacks the charisma to make it in Hollywood.

ALTRUISM

A rare and endangered species of behavior where individuals sacrifice their last slice of pizza for a friend.

AMATEUR

Someone who confidently takes on a task they have absolutely no skill or expertise in, like playing "Stairway to Heaven" on the guitar after one lesson.

AMAZON

An online marketplace where you can buy everything you've ever wanted, as long as you're okay with it being delivered in 47 separate packages.

AMNESIA

A convenient condition that allows politicians to forget campaign promises once elected.

ANGER

The emotion that turns you into a human volcano, spewing words and fiery glares at innocent bystanders.

ANKLE

A body part that's suspiciously easy to injure, rendering you temporarily disabled while prompting friends and colleagues to ask, "How on earth did you manage that?"

ANNOYANCE

The emotion you experience when your neighbor insists on mowing their lawn at 6 AM on a Sunday, or when someone chews gum with their mouth open.

ANTICIPATE

The art of looking forward to something so much that you inevitably jinx it and it gets canceled.

ANTIQUE

Old stuff you convince yourself is valuable while cluttering your home.

ANTIVIRUS

Software that constantly reminds you that your computer is more vulnerable than a paper mache fortress in a hailstorm.

ANTS

Tiny workaholics who coordinate picnics heists one crumb at a time, all while carrying their own body weight in snacks.

APOCALYPSE

The end of the world, often characterized by zombies, aliens, or a severe shortage of Wi-Fi.

APPLIANCES

The gadgets that you swear will make your life easier but actually just add more buttons to push and things to clean.

ARACHNOPHOBIA

A rational fear of eight-legged creatures that somehow manages to transform a sock on the floor into a tarantula in your mind.

ARROGANCE

The belief that you're the center of the universe, even though your only notable achievement is completing a 1000-piece jigsaw puzzle once.

ART

A subjective form of expression that turns stick figures into million-dollar masterpieces, depending on the artist's salesmanship.

ASPIRIN

A magical tablet that cures everything from headaches to existential crises, provided you don't exceed the recommended daily dose of 50.

ASTROLOGY

The cosmic belief system that claims your personality is determined by the position of the planets, not your Netflix preferences.

AUTOCORRECT

A modern form of linguistic sabotage designed to keep your texting life exciting and unpredictable.

AUTUMN

The season that heralds the return of pumpkin spice lattes, plaid flannel shirts, and endless debates about the proper pronunciation of "fall" vs. "autumn."

AWKWARD

The dance moves you pull when you're convinced you're the next Beyoncé but look more like a malfunctioning robot.

AXE

A tool that makes you feel like a lumberjack until you accidentally cut down your neighbor's prized rosebush.

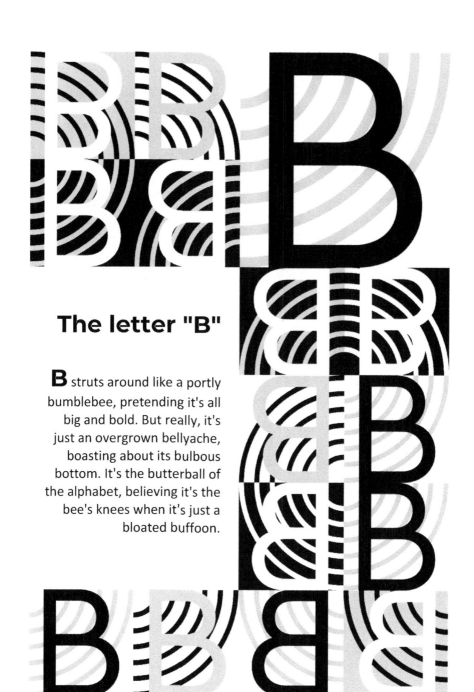

The letter "B"

B struts around like a portly bumblebee, pretending it's all big and bold. But really, it's just an overgrown bellyache, boasting about its bulbous bottom. It's the butterball of the alphabet, believing it's the bee's knees when it's just a bloated buffoon.

BABY

A tiny human who takes over your life, demands constant attention, and has the power to make you say things like, "Aww, did you go poo-poo?"

BACKPACK

A magical bag that's always bigger on the inside, until you need to find your keys.

BACON

A crispy, delicious reason why vegetarians always seem a little grumpy.

BAGUETTE

The edible weapon of choice for any aspiring French bread-sword fighter.

BALLET

An elegant dance form that requires years of training, grace, and the ability to balance on one toe while pretending not to be in pain.

BALLOON

A colorful bag of air that serves as a reminder that humans can get excited over the simplest things.

BANANA

Nature's portable telephone, complete with a peel for added protection.

BAND-AID

A small piece of adhesive that can heal wounds and mend broken hearts, but not always at the same time.

BANK

A place that lends you an umbrella when the sun is shining and demands it back when it starts raining.

BARBECUE

The culinary event where you attempt to tame fire and earn the title of Grill Master.

BASEBALL

A sport that involves hitting a ball with a stick and running in circles while the crowd screams.

BASKETBALL

A sport where people run around, throwing a ball through a hoop, all while pretending to not notice how tall some of them are.

BATHROOM

The private sanctuary where you ponder life's mysteries and lose epic battles against tangled toilet paper.

BEACH

The place where sand becomes your permanent accessory, and seagulls plot against your ice cream.

BEANIE

A magical hat that can generate static electricity in your hair, ensuring you'll look like you just stuck your finger in a light socket at all times.

BEARD

A facial accessory that provides warmth in winter, food storage in summer, and endless debate among those who argue whether you look more like a lumberjack or a hipster.

BED

The adult's time machine, instantly transporting you to the next day's problems.

BEER

An alcoholic beverage that somehow turns introverts into extroverts, extroverts into philosophers and everyone into terrible dancers.

BICYCLE

A two-wheeled contraption that offers a fantastic way to exercise, reduce your carbon footprint, and terrorize pedestrians while pretending to be a Tour de France champion.

BIGFOOT

The legendary creature known for its reclusive nature, mysterious footprints, and impeccable talent for avoiding smartphone cameras.

BIKINI

The daring swimwear that makes you feel fabulous and terrified all at once.

BILINGUAL

A person who claims to speak two languages fluently but often ends up ordering "bread with cheese" instead of a sophisticated dish in either language.

BIOHAZARD

A label used to identify things that are so dangerous, even germs are afraid to go near them.

BIRTHDAY

A reminder that you've successfully completed another orbit around the sun without getting abducted by aliens

BLANKET

The security cloak that transforms you into a burrito of comfort and procrastination.

BLENDER

A noisy tornado machine that turns innocent fruits and vegetables into liquid concoctions that you hope will taste better than they sound.

BOMBASTIC

The art of using unnecessarily big words to make yourself sound smarter, even when discussing something as simple as cereal preferences.

BONSAI

Tiny trees that look like they're training for a miniature forest Olympics.

BOOK

A portable portal to different worlds, often used to impress people when displayed on a bookshelf.

BOOKMARK

A slip of paper or fancy trinket used to mark your place in a book you haven't picked up in months.

BOOMERANG

An Australian invention designed to confuse and humble anyone who tries to throw it.

BOTOX

The magical potion that temporarily freezes your face in a way that suggests you're permanently surprised.

BRA

The undergarment that promises support but often becomes a medieval torture device.

BRAIN

The organ responsible for thoughts, memories, and the sudden urge to sing "Baby Shark" at inopportune moments.

BREAD

The staff of life that comes in countless shapes, sizes, and gluten-free varieties, but is always the first to disappear at a dinner party.

BREAKFAST

The most important meal of the day, unless you're running late, in which case, it's coffee.

BROCCOLI

The miniature trees of the vegetable world, often dismissed by children as inedible forest specimens.

BROOM

A broomstick with aspirations of becoming a wizard's staff, settling for sweeping up crumbs instead.

BUBBLEGUM

The sweet and chewy substance that gives you the superpower of blowing perfectly shaped bubbles, right before they inevitably pop all over your face.

BUCKET

A versatile container for hauling water, building sandcastles, or wearing as a makeshift helmet.

BUDGET

A mythical financial plan that crumbles the moment you see a "sale" sign or smell freshly baked cookies.

BUFFET

The ultimate test of self-control, where you attempt to load your plate with a little bit of everything, only to end up with a tower of food that rivals the Leaning Tower of Pisa.

BUG

Nature's tiny pranksters that buzz, bite, and find your picnic no matter where you hide it.

BULLY

Adult-sized toddler with the emotional intelligence of a rock and the empathy of a cactus.

BULLSEYE

The center of the target you always miss when trying to impress your friends at the carnival by winning that giant stuffed bear.

BUREAUCRACY

A system of government so efficient that even the simplest task requires a 47-page form and three visits to City Hall.

BURGER

A deliciously engineered food item that turns vegetarians into temporary carnivores.

BURGLAR

A nocturnal entrepreneur who offers a unique "home rearranging" service, specializing in helping you rediscover your hidden treasures by relocating them to their secret hideaway.

BUTTERFLY

A beautiful insect that spends most of its life as an ugly caterpillar, teaching us that beauty is a cruel and fleeting thing.

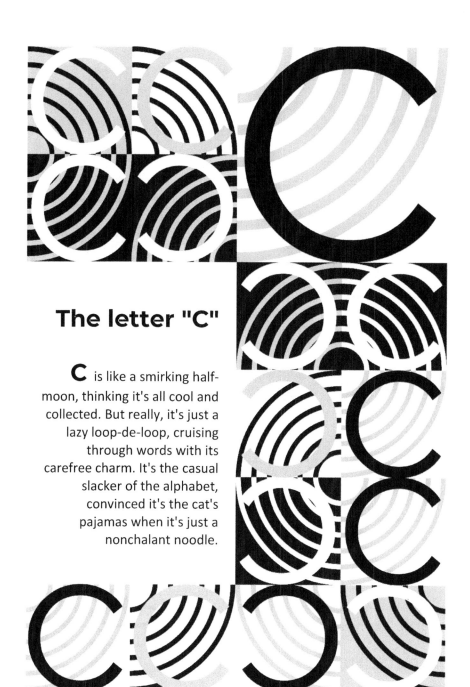

The letter "C"

C is like a smirking half-moon, thinking it's all cool and collected. But really, it's just a lazy loop-de-loop, cruising through words with its carefree charm. It's the casual slacker of the alphabet, convinced it's the cat's pajamas when it's just a nonchalant noodle.

CACTUS

Mother Nature's way of saying, "Don't touch me unless you want to regret it."

CAFFEINE

The legal drug of choice for people who prefer alertness over sleep.

CAKE

A dessert so so so irresistible that it has its own gravitational pull on your fork.

CALCULATOR

A pocket-sized genius that's great at math but clueless about the meaning of life.

CALENDAR

A tool that allows you to plan your life meticulously and then watch as your plans disintegrate into chaos.

CAMPERS

The tactical mastermind gamers who hide in corners, waiting to ambush unsuspecting foes, because patience is a virtue.

CANDLE

A source of romantic ambiance that doubles as a fire hazard, adding excitement to any evening.

CAPPUCCINO

Coffee art's canvas, where baristas turn foam into miniature sculptures that you'll hesitate to sip.

CAR

A metal beast that devours money through fuel, repairs, and parking fees.

CARROT

Nature's orange wand, famous for improving your eyesight and starring in Bugs Bunny's one-veggie show.

CASH

The elusive paper currency that disappears from your wallet at an alarming rate.

CAT

A furry overlord that alternates between ignoring you and plotting world domination.

CELEBRITY

Individuals famous for their exceptional talent in either acting, singing, or... getting married multiple times and attending parties?

CELLPHONE

The ultimate invention designed to keep you connected to the world and disconnected from the person sitting across from you.

CELLULITE

Your body's avant-garde art installation, completed with its own unique topographical map and textures added perfection.

CEMETERY

The ultimate retirement home, where residents never complain about the food or the neighbors.

CENSORSHIP

The act of protecting you from offensive content by blacking out all the interesting parts.

CHAMELEON

The shape-shifting reptile that puts your adaptability skills to shame.

CHAMPION

Someone who excels at something, leaving the rest of us to question if we're even participating in the same competition or just watching a different game entirely.

CHAOS

The natural state of your sock drawer and the universe in general

CHEATS

The magical codes in video games that turn you into an invincible, flying, unlimited-ammo-having superhero, just because you're tired of losing.

CHEESECAKE

The dessert that's basically an excuse to eat a whole block of cream cheese with a sugar disguise.

CHESS

A battle of wits where you move miniature armies while pretending not to be devastated by your opponent's superior strategy.

CHICKEN

Feathered alarm clock with questionable intelligence, known for their daily concerts at the crack of dawn.

CHILI

A spicy dish that reminds you that your taste buds exist, often followed by a desperate search for milk or yogurt to cool the fiery rebellion in your mouth.

CHOCOLATE

The solution to all of life's problems until you realize you've eaten an entire bar and your problems are now multiplied by guilt and calories.

CHOPSTICKS

Elegant utensils that make eating a noodle soup look like an Olympic event in dexterity and patience.

CIDER

The beverage that makes you question why you ever settled for boring old apple juice.

CLOCK

A device that relentlessly measures the passage of time, reminding you that you're never as punctual as you promised yourself you'd be.

CLOWN

The performer who terrifies as many children as they amuse, all while wearing oversized shoes.

COCKROACH

Earth's ultimate survivor, with a unique talent for disappearing when you turn on the lights.

COFFEE

A magical elixir that transforms groggy zombies into semi-functional humans.

COINCIDENCE

The phenomenon that makes you question the universe's sense of humor when you run into your ex at the grocery store while buying copious amounts of ice cream.

COLD

A contagious condition that turns your nose into a leaky faucet and your body into a whiny mess.

COLLEGE

A place where you pay a fortune to learn that you should've paid more attention in high school.

COMEDY

The art of making people laugh, often achieved by pointing out the absurdity of everyday life, like how you always manage to pick the slowest line at the grocery store.

COMPASS

The tiny instrument of geometry that can draw perfect circles or accidentally stab you in the leg.

COMPLAINING

The universal language of humanity, often employed when the weather is too hot, too cold, or just too "weather-y" in general.

COMPUTER

A device that has revolutionized procrastination and allowed you to waste time more efficiently.

CONFETTI

Tiny paper shrapnel that litters your life after celebrations, mocking your cleaning skills.

CONFUSION

The state where your brain resembles a tangled slinky, and you wonder if you accidentally put salt in your coffee.

CONSTRUCTION

The process of fixing one pothole while creating three more, leading you to wonder if roadwork is just a modern form of performance art.

COOKIES

The bite-sized rounds of temptation that somehow disappear within minutes of leaving the oven.

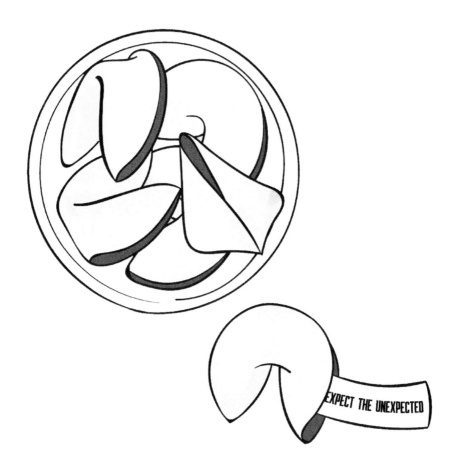

**Oh, how original!
Maybe next time, this cookie
will predict your predictability.**

COUCH

A piece of furniture that transforms you into a sloth and a detective, as you search for the remote control that's always hiding.

COUCHSURFING

A travel trend where you stay with strangers for free, all while hoping they're not secretly plotting to harvest your organs.

COUSIN

The relative you see once a year, just long enough to forget how you're related.

COW

Nature's four-legged milk-producing machine, designed to turn grass into beverages that are utterly lacking in lactose intolerance consideration.

CRAYON

A waxy stick of vibrant color that serves as a child's first artistic tool and an adult's last resort for labeling moving boxes.

CUCUMBER

A seemingly innocent vegetable that becomes the prime suspect when your salad suddenly tastes terrible.

CURIOSITY

The insatiable urge to know everything about something until you accidentally fall down an internet rabbit hole and forget what you were originally curious about.

The ability to awaken the mere mortals, who lack celestial taste buds, is truly remarkable. One sip, and we're transported to a realm of unparalleled divinity, or so we'd like to believe.

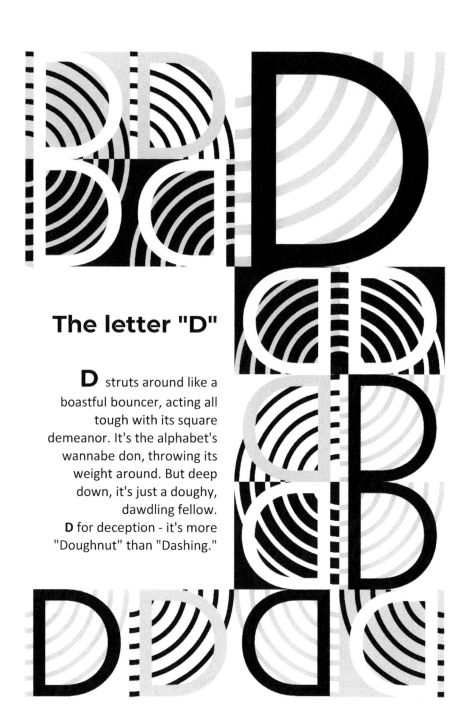

The letter "D"

D struts around like a boastful bouncer, acting all tough with its square demeanor. It's the alphabet's wannabe don, throwing its weight around. But deep down, it's just a doughy, dawdling fellow.
D for deception - it's more "Doughnut" than "Dashing."

DABBING

The contemporary dance move that makes you look like you're sneezing into your elbow while trying to assert your dominance on the dance floor.

DALMATIAN

The dog breed that convinced everyone that owning 101 of them would be a good idea, despite the inevitable chaos and endless fur.

DANCE

The art of moving your body rhythmically to music, often resembling a cross between a seizure and an attempt to dislodge an invisible scorpion from your pants.

DANDELION

The flower who has the audacity to say: "I dare you to try and get rid of me! Or make a wish."

DANDRUFF

Your scalp is a imaginary snow globe, and it's time for a shake, right on your shoulders.

DARTS

The pub game that turns throwing sharp objects at a wall into a legitimate sport, as long as you don't hit anyone.

DATING

The process of finding out how many hobbies and interests you can pretend to share before revealing your true self.

DEADLINE

The ultimate motivator, forcing you to complete a week's worth of work in the last five minutes.

DEATH

The one thing in life that's truly inevitable, often leaving you with deep philosophical questions, like "What happens to my Netflix subscription?"

DEBATE

The sport where people passionately argue their opinions while secretly hoping they can change their opponent's mind with the power of words.

DECORATION

The process of turning your living space into a Pinterest-worthy masterpiece, only to have your cat knock everything over within seconds.

DEER

The forest's answer to car accidents, always appearing out of nowhere just in time to test your brakes.

DELIVERY

The service that promises to bring you food in 30 minutes but somehow arrives in either 5 minutes or 5 hours.

DENTIST

A licensed sadist who insists on poking sharp objects into your mouth while you can't protest.

DENTURES

The solution to losing your teeth, allowing you to chew food again and terrify small children with a gummy grin.

DESPERATION

The emotion that strikes when your phone battery hits 1% and there's no charger in sight, as if it's the end of civilization.

DIAPER

A humble yet essential piece of parenting equipment that transforms your sweet bundle of joy into a ticking time bomb of biohazard.

DICTIONARY

A heavy book filled with words you don't know, which is why you look them up online instead.

DIET

A temporary state of self-denial followed by an inevitable reunion with your favorite comfort foods.

DINOSAUR

Giant reptiles from the past, also known as Mother Nature's first attempt at creating movie monsters.

DISGUST

The reaction to discovering an expired yogurt container in the back of your fridge, with a side of dramatic gagging.

Dinosaurs thought they had time too.

DISHES

The endless cycle of dirty to clean to dirty again, proving that Sisyphus might have had it easy.

DISHONESTY

The art of bending the truth to the point where it's doing yoga poses that no one ever thought possible.

DISTRACTING

The intentional act of diverting someone's attention, often utilized by pets, children, and coworkers during important Zoom meetings.

DJ

A musical maestro who believes every song can be improved with the strategic placement of an air horn sound effect.

DOCTOR

A person who kills your ills with pills then kills you with bills.

DOG

A loyal companion who thinks your socks are a delicacy and that every passing mail carrier is a mortal enemy.

DOLPHIN

Aquatic show-off with a knack for stealing the spotlight and making humans feel inadequate in the water.

DOMESTICATION

The process that transforms wild creatures into pets, leaving you to wonder if they secretly miss the days of hunting and foraging.

DONKEY

The hardworking and stubborn creature that's basically the spirit animal of anyone who's ever tried to assemble IKEA furniture.

DOODLE

The absentminded scribbles that populate the margins of your notes, a silent protest against boredom and meetings that could've been emails.

DOPPELGÄNGER

The person who looks exactly like you and makes you question if you're living in a parallel universe or just part of a cosmic joke.

DORMITORY

The shared living space where you learn to coexist with strangers, surviving on instant noodles.

DOUBT

The thing that creeps in just as you're about to make a major life decision, asking, "Are you sure about this?"

DOUGHNUT

A sugary torus of temptation, convincing you that one won't hurt until you find yourself surrounded by a sea of empty wrappers.

DRACULA

The world's most famous vampire, who realized that eternal life isn't as glamorous when you can't enjoy garlic bread.

DRAGON

The mythical creature that can fly, breathe fire, and somehow has a better resume than most job applicants.

DRAMA

The art of making life's smallest inconveniences sound like the plot of a Shakespearean tragedy.

DRAWING

The art of convincing yourself that the squiggles on paper are indeed a masterpiece, while everyone else is just trying to figure out what you were attempting to create.

DREADLOCKS

A hairstyle that requires you to stop combing your hair for a year and results in looking like you have your own personal bird's nest.

DRIVEWAY

The designated space for your car, which somehow always ends up being the preferred spot for neighborhood kids to play basketball.

DRIVING

An activity that transforms even the calmest individuals into enraged traffic warriors who communicate primarily through hand gestures.

DRIZZLE

The meteorological equivalent of a leaky faucet, where the sky can't make up its mind if it's raining or not.

DRONE

The robotic flying device that captures breathtaking aerial views and terrifies every bird within a five-mile radius.

DROWNING

The dramatic reenactment you perform every time you step into a pool and momentarily forget how to swim.

DROWSY

That state of being where you're neither fully asleep nor awake, but instead stuck in a limbo of nonsensical thoughts and pillow drool.

DUCK

A bird that waddles, quacks, and occasionally appears on your dinner plate as a crispy delicacy.

DUMPSTER

The urban treasure chest where one person's trash is another person's treasure, unless it's just actual trash, in which case, it's everyone's trash.

DUST

The magical substance that appears on all surfaces the moment you finish cleaning, as if mocking your efforts

.

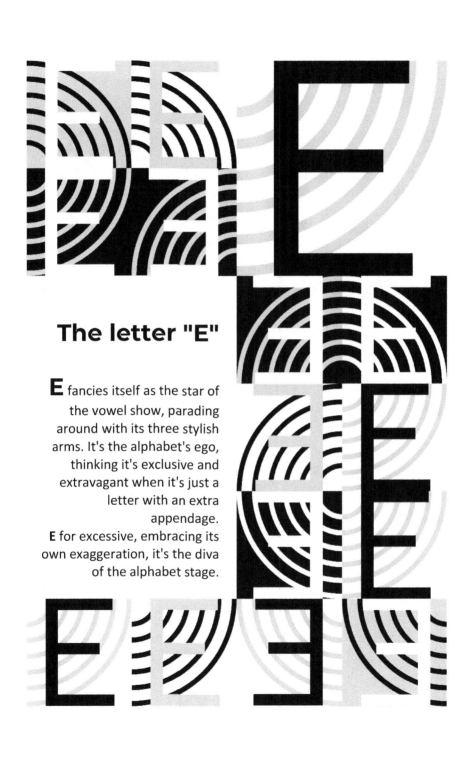

The letter "E"

E fancies itself as the star of the vowel show, parading around with its three stylish arms. It's the alphabet's ego, thinking it's exclusive and extravagant when it's just a letter with an extra appendage.
E for excessive, embracing its own exaggeration, it's the diva of the alphabet stage.

EAGER

The state of being excitedly impatient about something that will probably disappoint you.

EAGLE

A majestic bird that looks down upon all other birds, mostly because it can fly higher.

EARTHQUAKE

When Mother Earth decides it's time for a little shimmy and shake to remind us who is boss.

EAVESDROPPING

The fine art of pretending to read a book or magazine while secretly listening to someone else's juicy conversation.

E-BOOK

The digital version of a book that's excellent for the environment but lacks the satisfying smell and heft of a physical book.

ECHO

The universe's way of confirming that you talk to yourself too much.

ECONOMICS

The art of making predictions about the future while blaming the past.

EDGE

The place where you're one step away from brilliance or a trip to the hospital.

EDIBLE

Anything that can be eaten without calling 911 afterward.

EDUCATION

The process of learning things you'll forget as soon as the final exam is over.

ELATION

The ecstatic emotion that makes you feel like you've won the lottery, even if it's just a free coffee.

ELBOW

The body's built-in tool for accidentally knocking over everything on a table, resulting in a lightning bolt of pain.

ELECTION

A process where politicians promise the moon, the stars, and free WiFi for all, and then deliver none of the above.

ELECTRICIAN

The person who always turns off the power right when you're about to win an online game.

ELEPHANT

The earth's original bulldozer with built-in air conditioning, equipped to turn any water source into a luxurious spa.

ELEVATE

The art of making a regular sandwich sound gourmet by calling it a "deconstructed culinary masterpiece."

ELEVATOR

A metal box that forces you to stand shoulder-to-shoulder with strangers, united by a common goal: avoiding eye contact.

EMAIL

A modern form of communication where you can send important messages and receive 10,000 unimportant ones in return.

EMBARRASSMENT

The feeling you get when your stomach starts making strange noises in a silent room.

EMPATHY

The ability to understand and share the feelings of others, unless they're in line in front of you at the grocery store.

EMPLOYEE

The skilled multitasker who can simultaneously complete their assigned tasks, navigate office politics, and master the art of looking busy even when there's nothing to do.

ENTHUSIASM

The mysterious force that compels you to start a new hobby every two weeks.

EMERGENCY BOX

EPIDEMIC

When your laughter becomes so contagious that people start avoiding you.

ERASERS

Tiny pink rectangles that make your mistakes vanish, but only if you rub them vigorously enough.

ERGONOMICS

The scientific study of how many different positions you can sit in before your chair wins.

ERROR

The force that makes your autocorrect change "I'm on my way" to "I'm on my whale."

ERUPTION

When your cat finally loses its cool and knocks over all your houseplants.

ETCETERA

The Latin word that means "I'm too lazy to list everything, but you get the idea."

ETERNITY

The grand masterpiece of waiting, where time stands still, and boredom reigns supreme. It's like watching paint dry, but with the added bonus of never getting to see the finished product.

EUROVISION

The annual competition where countries battle it out to see who can write the catchiest song about vegetables.

EVAPORATION

The process that turns your ice cream into a sad, melted puddle of disappointment, reminding you that all good things in life eventually disappear

EVEREST

The mountain that proves humans will climb anything as long as there's a "world's tallest" title at stake.

EVOLUTION

The theory that suggests we all started as single-celled organisms and somehow evolved into creatures who waste hours watching cat videos.

EX

A former lover who conveniently resurfaces when you're finally happy with someone else.

EXAGGERATE

The art of making your story so unbelievably epic that even dragons take notes.

EXASPERATE

The feeling you get when you can't find your glasses, and they're perched on your head.

IN CASE OF FIRE
EXIT BUILDING BEFORE
TWEETING ABOUT IT

EXCLAMATION

The punctuation mark used to convey excitement, because CAPS LOCK wasn't enough.

EXERCISE

The art of voluntarily putting your body through pain and suffering, all in the pursuit of that elusive "summer body" that seems to hide year-round.

EXFOLIATE

The skincare ritual that convinces you that scrubbing your face with sandpaper will lead to eternal youth.

EXHAUSTION

The feeling you have on a long Monday, causing you to question whether you have the energy to even microwave leftovers.

EXIT

The only thing you look for in a store when you almost stumble into an old relative.

EYEBROW

The expressive caterpillars that live on your forehead and signal your emotions to the world.

EYEROLL

A full-body workout that happens when someone says something utterly ridiculous.

Expert Multitasker:

A person who can brilliantly divide their attention between tasks, ensuring that every task receives a fair share of their confusion and none of their undivided focus.

The letter "F"

F struts around like a feathered diva in the alphabet's fashion show. It's the flamboyant peacock, thinking it's fabulous with its curvy strut, but it's just a flimsy facade, all feathers, and no flight.
F is for faux fabulousness, fooling us with its foppish flair.

FACEBOOK

The place where you pretend to have a social life while sitting in your pajamas.

FACEPALM

The universal gesture for "I can't believe you just said that."

FAIRYTALE

A story where everything is perfect, except for the dragons, witches, and evil stepmothers.

FALCON

A bird so majestic that it can hunt from the sky and still look cooler than you on a hoverboard.

FAMILY

The group of people who will criticize you at the dinner table and defend you to the death outside of it.

FANATIC

A person who takes their obsessions to the next level, like knowing the star sign of their favorite cereal mascot.

FANTASTIC

A word you use to describe a mediocre movie when you don't want to hurt your friend's feelings.

FARMVILLE

The digital place where you can grow crops, build a virtual empire, and ignore your actual chores.

FASHION

The art of wearing clothes that make you look like you're trying not to look like you're trying and that uncomfortable is the new comfortable.

FEAR

The sensation that makes you jump at shadows and believe your own hairbrush is a deadly snake.

FEARLESS

The state of mind you achieve when you're brave enough to confront the spider in your bathtub.

FEBRUARY

The shortest month that still manages to feel the longest.

FEDORA

The official hat of people who think they look good in hats but don't.

FEEDBACK

The reassuring sound your cat makes while scratching your new leather couch.

FEET

A device used for finding LEGOs in the dark.

FELINE

A fancy way of saying "cat," because cats deserve fancy names.

FEROCIOUS

How you describe your appetite when you haven't eaten for a whole hour.

FERTILIZER

A bag of lies you spread on your lawn in the vain hope that it will become as green as your neighbor's.

FIDDLE

The musical instrument that makes you look cool when you play it but sound like a cat being strangled when you're learning.

FILTER

A magical tool that can turn even the most mundane selfie into a masterpiece suitable for a museum.

FINALE

The long-awaited episode that ends your favorite TV show, leaving you with an empty bag of chips and emotionally unprepared for real life.

FINANCE

The art of spending 90% of your life working to afford a house you're rarely in because you're always working

FINGERPAINT

The art form you mastered in kindergarten, but still can't quite get right

FIREFIGHTER

The brave soul who saves cats from trees while looking cool in a uniform.

FIREWORKS

Explosive pyrotechnics that light up the night sky, impressing everyone except your dog, who thinks the world is ending.

FISHBOWL

The glass container that turns your pet fish into an unintentional spectator at all family gatherings.

FITNESS

A term used by gym enthusiasts to make the rest of us feel guilty for eating that second donut.

FLATTERY

The art of making someone feel good about themselves just before asking for a favor

FLEA

The tiny jumping nuisance that turns your pet into a personal trampoline.

FLIRTATION

The subtle art of making someone feel attractive while leaving them in a state of confusion about your intentions.

FLOSS

The tiny string that wages war against spinach, meat, and your dignity.

FLUORESCENT

The lighting that can make even the most attractive person look like they just emerged from a swamp.

FLY

The insect equivalent of a forgetful doorbell, buzzing around aimlessly until it finds the nearest window.

FOIL

The culinary tool that turns your leftovers into a kitchen origami project.

FOOTBALL

A sport where people chase a ball for 90 minutes, ending in a thrilling 0-0 tie.

FOREHEAD

The part of your face that somehow attracts furniture corners.

FORK

A pronged utensil designed to make eating more efficient, yet somehow fails miserably when it comes to spaghetti.

FOSSIL

A rock with an identity crisis, convinced it used to be something cooler.

FOUNTAIN

A water feature that dares you to drink from it, despite the signs saying not to.

FOX

A cunning creature that steals chickens and your heart simultaneously.

FRIDAY

The day that proves time is a construct, as it feels both endless and over in a flash.

FRUSTRATION

What you feel when the USB plug won't go in on the first and second time.

FUGITIVE

The person who escapes from a boring party without saying goodbye.

FUN

The elusive concept you keep hearing about but can't seem to find amidst your adult responsibilities.

FUNKY

The level of groove you reach when you put on mismatched socks and embrace it as a fashion statement.

FURNITURE

Inanimate objects that secretly conspire to stub your toes, catch your shins, and ruin your life, one bruise at a time.

Forgive and forget?
I'm neither Jesus
nor do I have Alzheimer's.

The letter "G"

G struts around like a hipster with a curly mustache, thinking it's got some unique edge. It's the alphabet's goofy guru, flaunting its loopy tail like a fancy fashion statement. **G** stands for grandiosity, but it's really just a glorified pretzel with a pretentious twist!

GADGET

A small device that you can't live without, until it malfunctions, at which point you wonder why you ever bought it.

GALAXY

A massive collection of stars, planets, and cosmic mysteries that exist solely to make your selfies look more dramatic.

GAMBLING

The art of voluntarily throwing your money into a pit and hoping it magically multiplies.

GARAGE

A space originally designed for cars but now reserved for all the things you don't know where to put.

GARDENING

The art of growing plants, killing them, and then blaming the weather

GARLIC

Nature's way of telling you to social distance after consuming a meal.

GASOLINE

The overpriced elixir that powers your car and ensures you spend more time at the pump than with loved ones.

GARBAGE CAN

GAZELLE

A graceful creature that exists to remind us that we, as humans, will never look as elegant when we run.

GELATO

The Italian word for "ice cream," which somehow tastes even better when you say it with an accent.

GENEROSITY

The act of giving someone the last slice of pizza while secretly plotting their demise.

GENETICS

The science that explains why you look like a weird blend of your parents, minus the good parts.

GENIE

A magical being that grants you three wishes but then spends the entire time passive-aggressively reminding you of the limitations.

GENIUS

A person who claims they're a genius, usually right before doing something incredibly dumb.

GENTLEMAN

An endangered species that opens doors for others, says "please" and "thank you," and may soon only exist in history books.

GEOGRAPHY

The subject that teaches you where countries are located, just in case you ever decide to win a game of "Name That Capital."

GEOMETRY

The math class that makes you question the usefulness of shapes you'll never encounter in real life.

GESTURE

The hand movement you make when you're trying to explain directions in a foreign country, ensuring you end up in a completely different place.

GHOST

The invisible roommate who thinks it's hilarious to rearrange your furniture while you sleep.

GIF

A brief, looping video that's the perfect response when words are just too much effort.

GIFT

The item you spend hours choosing, only for the recipient to pretend they like it and then re-gift it to someone else.

GIGABYTE

A unit of digital storage that makes you wonder why you can't fit your entire life into one of these.

GIGANTIC

The polite way of saying "absurdly huge," often used when describing the pile of laundry on your chair.

GIMME

The word that transforms you from a polite human into a grabby toddler when offered free food.

GINGERBREAD

The cookie that tempts you into building gingerbread houses, only to realize that architectural design isn't your strong suit.

GIRAFFE

A creature with an impossibly long neck and a heartwarming dedication to making you feel inadequate about your inability to reach high shelves.

GIRLFRIEND

The person who knows your flaws but chooses to keep you around anyway (at least until they don't). Also see: **BOYFRIEND.**

GIVEAWAY

A contest that promises prizes but often results in a surplus of promotional emails in your inbox.

GLITTER

The herpes of the craft world, guaranteed to stick around for years after the party is over.

GLUE

The gooey adhesive that bonds paper together, your fingers to everything, and sometimes your sanity to the edge of your desk.

GLUTTONY

A hobby where you try to fit as much food as possible into your stomach, often accompanied by regret.

GNOME

Tiny, bearded creature that mysteriously appear in gardens, probably to judge your choice of flowers.

GOGGLES

The eyewear that transforms you into a sci-fi superhero while simultaneously making you look like a confused insect.

GOLF

A sport where you chase a tiny ball around for hours and celebrate the one time you get it in the hole.

GOOGLE

The search engine that knows your deepest secrets, yet still manages to show you ads for things you don't want.

GORILLA

A creature that proves even in the animal kingdom, muscles and a hairy chest are still considered attractive.

GOULASH

A stew that's basically a culinary experiment to see how many ingredients can fit into one pot before it becomes unrecognizable.

GOURMET

A fancy way of saying "expensive," usually accompanied by tiny portions and lots of foam.

GPS

A device that provides directions to places you didn't know existed, then politely insults you when you make a wrong turn.

GRADUATION

The art of wearing an oversized hat and robe ceremony, to celebrates your academic achievements.

GRAMMAR

The rules that separate those who write "your" instead of "you're" from the rest of humanity.

GRAPEFRUIT

The fruit that tricks you into thinking it's sweet, only to unleash its tart vengeance with every bite.

GRASSHOPPER

A leggy daredevil that practices Olympic-level jumps, just for the thrill of it.

GRATITUDE

The warm, fuzzy feeling that emerges when someone lets you have the last slice of pizza without a fight.

GRAVITY

The force that keeps you grounded, except when you trip over your own shoelaces.

GREED

The strong belief that you need a bigger TV, even though your current one is already the size of a wall.

GROOMING

The daily struggle of making yourself look presentable, only to end up looking exactly the same as before.

GRUMBLE

The noise you make when you're pretending to be upset but secretly enjoying the attention.

GUIDEBOOK

The book you buy before a trip and never read until you're hopelessly lost in a foreign city.

GUM

A chewy confection that doubles as a social deterrent when you accidentally pop it too loudly in a silent room.

Don't study sarcastic people, you will never graduate.

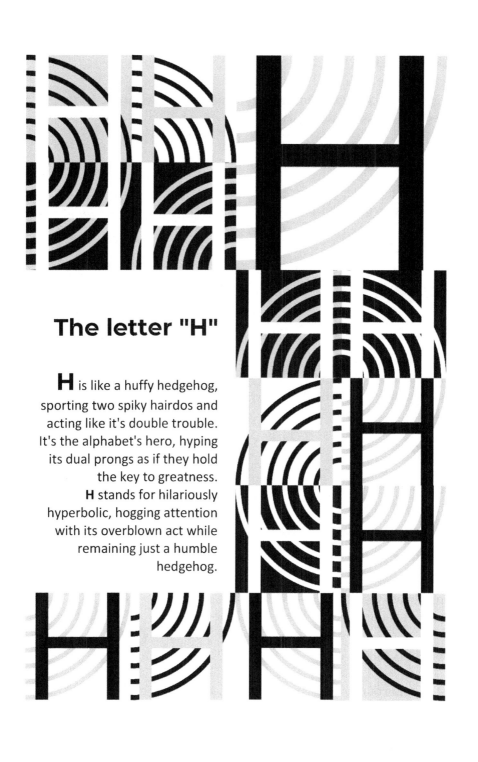

The letter "H"

H is like a huffy hedgehog, sporting two spiky hairdos and acting like it's double trouble. It's the alphabet's hero, hyping its dual prongs as if they hold the key to greatness. **H** stands for hilariously hyperbolic, hogging attention with its overblown act while remaining just a humble hedgehog.

HAIRBALL

A mysterious, cat-produced object that materializes when you least expect it, like a furry alien invasion.

HAIRBRUSH

A tool designed to tame your unruly locks into submission, inevitably causing you to question whether you've just created a nest on your head.

HAIRCUT

The magical procedure that makes you 100% more attractive, as long as you avoid looking in the mirror immediately afterward.

HAIRDRYER

A loud wind machine that helps you achieve that "stuck-your-finger-in-an-electrical-socket" look.

HALF

The convenient fraction that suggests you're making progress when you've actually just divided your problems in two and are still stuck with both.

HAMMER

The ultimate tool that turns every DIY project into a test of patience and hand-eye coordination.

HAMMOCK

The epitome of relaxation until you try to get in and end up tangled in a cocoon of fabric.

HAMSTER

The small, furry creature that runs tirelessly on its wheel, teaching you the invaluable life lesson that no matter how much effort you exert, you'll end up exactly where you started.

HANDBAG

A stylish accessory that, when opened, reveals a parallel universe where everything but the one item you urgently need resides.

HANDCUFFS

Metal restraints designed for law enforcement but frequently used in amateur magic tricks, intimate role-play, and awkward situations at frat parties.

HANDSHAKE

The old-school ritual to show signs of respect, by exchanging germs with strangers while maintaining eye contact to establish dominance.

HANGOVER

The body's revenge for the fun you had last night, serving as a reminder that you're no longer 21.

HAPPINESS

The feeling that convinces you the world is a Disney movie, and you're the main character.

HARP

The angelic instrument that, in the hands of amateurs, sounds more like a cat in distress.

HAT

The fashion accessory you wear to make an extravagant statement about your hairstyle, just before it flattens your hair into submission, ensuring your look is as dramatic as possible.

HEADPHONES

A suggestive way of saying: "I'm not listening to you, but I don't want to be rude about it."

HEADSHOT

The divine act of shooting someone in the face, virtually speaking, of course.

HEATWAVE

A phenomenon that turns your once-green lawn into a crispy potato chip and your A/C unit into your new best friend.

HEAVEN

A place that seems to get further away as humans scientific knowledge improves

HECTIC

A state of existence where every minute is a thrilling race against the clock, and your to-do list magically multiplies faster than rabbits on caffeine.

HEDGEHOG

A small, prickly creature that secretly enjoys popping balloons when no one is looking.

In Heaven, they say, it's all joy and song,
Harp-strumming angels, you can't go wrong.
Endless happiness, not a care in the air,
Sounds like a blast, if you're into that fare.

But Hell's a party that never will cease,
Elevator music, no sign of peace.
Hot wings aplenty, a fiery carnival ride,
Choose your destination, with nowhere to hide.

So, Heaven or Hell, the choice is yours to make,
In this cosmic comedy, for eternity's sake!

HELICOPTER

The vehicle that combines the grace of a mosquito with the noise of a rock concert.

HELLO

The socially mandated opening act of a conversation, designed to make you question the sincerity of every subsequent word exchanged.

HELMET

The head accessory designed to make you look like a sci-fi hero while attempting to protect your head from minor inconveniences like low doorframes... and gravity.

HICCUPS

Nature's way of making you sound like a confused baby seal, one involuntary "hic" at a time.

HIGH HEELS

The footwear that makes you feel both powerful and terrified with each step.

HIGHLIGHTERS

Neon weapons of mass distraction, used to create a rainbow explosion on your study materials.

HIPPOPOTAMUS

Nature's way of saying, "Let's make a creature that's both massive and oddly adorable."

HISTORY

The fascinating practice of learning about past mistakes while inexplicably repeating them with absolute confidence.

HITCHHIKER

The brave soul who believes getting a ride from strangers is a great life choice.

HOCKEY

A sport where grown adults chase a puck with sticks while wearing blades on their feet, somehow without turning it into a bloodbath.

HOME

The place where you spend half your life searching for your misplaced keys, only to find them in the most obvious spot you checked three times already.

HOMEWORK

A diabolical plot by teachers to ensure that students never have a moment of free time.

HONEYMOON

The vacation that follows the world's most stressful party, also known as a wedding.

HOPE

The magical belief that everything will turn out perfectly, despite overwhelming evidence to the contrary.

HORIZON

The elusive line that tempts you to chase after it, only to reveal that no matter how far you go, it will keep playing hard to get, ensuring your eternal pursuit of the unattainable.

HOROSCOPE

The daily dose of vague predictions that convinces you your lucky number is definitely 7. Or maybe 8.

HOSPITALITY

The art of inviting guests into your home and secretly hoping they cancel at the last minute so you can enjoy your personal space in peace.

HOTDOG

A cylindrical mystery meat that defies all logic by fitting into a bun, causing existential questions at every bite.

HOTEL

A temporary home where you collect tiny shampoo bottles as souvenirs and pretend to be a rich person for a few days.

HOUSEPLANT

A green companion that thrives on neglect and silently judges your watering skills.

HUGGABLE

A quality possessed by teddy bears, puppies, and people who've recently taken a shower.

HUMIDITY

The strong sensation of walking through a warm bowl of soup.

HUMOR

The elusive quality that makes you laugh at jokes while simultaneously questioning.... why you find them funny in the first place.

HUNGRY

The state of being where even a stale cracker starts to look like gourmet cuisine.

HYDRATION

The elusive goal of drinking enough water, often thwarted by your affinity for caffeinated beverages.

HYENA

A funny animal that laughs hysterically at its own jokes, reminding you that you're not the only one with a questionable sense of humor.

HYGIENE

The practice that separates humans from wild animals, unless it's a three-day camping trip.

HYPOCRISY

The fine art of preaching one thing while practicing another, because consistency is clearly overrated.

Happiness, that elusive quest we chase,
Like a snail's race in a never-ending space.
It's the pot of gold that leprechauns protect,
Or the winning lottery ticket we'd all select.

In life's absurdity, we still give it a try,
Happiness, you sly rogue, always waving goodbye!

The letter "I"

I is like a vain exclamation mark, standing tall and shouting "**Look at me!**" It's the alphabet's attention-seeker, insisting on its singular significance. "I" believes it's an island of importance, but really, it's just a straight line with delusions of grandeur. It's all about itself, inordinately and insanely.

IBUPROFEN

The medicine that makes you believe you're invincible until you try to move and leaves you longing for a lifetime prescription.

ICEBERG

Nature's game of peek-a-boo, where the majority remains hidden beneath the surface, just waiting to ruin a ship's day.

IDEA

The elusive muse that visits you in the shower but never sticks around long enough for you to write it down.

IDIOT

The true connoisseur of life's simplest mistakes, the Picasso of poor decisions, and the undisputed champion of accidental comedy.

IDLE

The ultimate state of productivity where nothing gets done but daydreams flourish.

IGLOO

An architecturally impressive snow fort that proves you don't need a degree to build a home in freezing conditions.

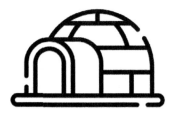

IGNITE

The spontaneous combustion of frustration that occurs when technology refuses to cooperate.

GREAT IDEAS START SMALL

IGNORANT

The delightful state of being where you don't need evidence because you're just right.

IGUANA

Nature's attempt at a pet dinosaur that couldn't quite commit to the role.

IMMACULATE

The state of cleanliness that lasts approximately five minutes after you finish tidying up.

IMMATURE

A word used by boring people to describe fun people

IMMORTALITY

The eternal joy of never having an excuse to retire, because even after a millennium, your boss still wants that report on their desk by Friday.

IMPATIENT

The feeling that arises when your computer takes more than three seconds to load a webpage.

IMPULSE

The brilliant idea that strikes you when you have no time to think, leading to questionable decisions like buying unnecessary kitchen gadgets or adopting a pet rock.

INBOX

The mysterious black hole where important emails go to hide, only to resurface when it's too late.

INCOGNITO

The stealth mode of the internet, used when you're shopping for surprise gifts and not Googling embarrassing symptoms.

INCOMPLETE

The assignment you turn in with utmost confidence, convinced that the teacher will appreciate your minimalist approach to deadlines.

INCONVENIENCE

What happens when you forget your phone charger, and you're forced to speak to your co-travelers instead.

INDEPENDENCE

The aspiration to stand on your own two feet, right up until the moment you need your parents to bail you out.

INDESTRUCTIBLE

An object's claim that it will never break, right before shattering into a million pieces at the slightest touch.

INDIFFERENCE

The emotion you choose when you can't decide between love and hate.

INDULGENT

The art of treating yourself so excessively that even your credit card sends you a "slow down" warning.

INEFFICIENCY

The baffling phenomenon where it takes longer to explain a task than to do it yourself.

INEPT

The polite way to describe someone who couldn't find water if they fell out of a boat.

INEVITABLE

The reminder that life's surprises are as predictable as your cat knocking over that precarious stack of books or mugs for the umpteenth time.

INFAMOUS

The title bestowed upon people who just couldn't resist being exceptionally bad at staying out of trouble.

INFLAMMABLE

The word that proves English enjoys setting traps for unsuspecting non-native speakers, because who doesn't want a language where "inflammable" means the same thing as "flammable"?

INFLATION

The economic phenomenon that turns your money into glorified Monopoly cash, just with more zeros.

INSECT

Nature's reminder that even the tiniest creatures can ruin a picnic.

INSECURITY

The nagging feeling that you'll never be good enough, no matter how many Instagram filters you apply.

INSINUATE

The art of suggesting something without actually saying it, leading to an infinite loop of misunderstandings.

INSOMNIA

The nocturnal curse that transforms your bed into a trampoline and your thoughts into a relentless carnival.

INSPIRATION

The elusive spark that conveniently appears when you least expect it and vanishes when you need it most.

INSTANT

The big big big biiiiiig promise that everything can be yours right now, except for patience and self-control.

INSTRUCTIONS

The guidelines you receive with any new purchase, which you promptly ignore until you've thoroughly messed up the assembly.

INSULT

The eloquent expression of your true feelings, usually aimed at someone who had the audacity to disagree with you.

INSURANCE

The money you pay to protect yourself from unforeseen disasters, which often feels like paying for permission to be unlucky.

INTERNET

The global playground where cat videos reign supreme and information can be found between memes.

INTERVIEW

The high-stress situation where you pretend to be the ideal candidate for a job you're secretly not sure you want.

INTROVERT

A person who recharges by being alone, except when they have to explain their introverted nature to extroverts.

INVENTION

The clever idea you had that will change the world, or at least until you realize someone else already patented it.

INVESTIGATOR

The modern-day Sherlock, uncovering the shocking truth that your pen was, in fact, just hiding behind your ear the entire time.

IRON

The appliance that takes up precious closet space just to press clothes you'll inevitably wrinkle again.

IRONY

The feeling of reading satirical dictionary entries while secretly enjoying them.

IRREPARABLE

The state of your favorite mug after it met your kitchen floor. Rest in pieces.

IRREPLACEABLE

There's no one else in the world who can do what you do, ask your cat.

IRRITATION

The heartwarming sensation that occurs when someone repeatedly asks you if you're irritated.

ISLAND

A remote paradise where you can escape from the world's problems until you realize that Wi-Fi is non-existent and sunscreen is mandatory.

ITCHY

The delightful sensation that makes you question if you've been bitten by invisible ants.

IVORY

The color that makes you realize how bad you are at keeping things clean.

The irony
of despising math like cat despises water, yet when it's time to count money, we become mathematical connoisseurs, savoring each equation like a fine wine.

The letter "J"

J is like a rebellious fishhook, always trying to snag the spotlight in the alphabet's ocean. It's the joker in the deck, flashing its curvy grin while hiding a quirky secret. J stands for jocular jackassery, hijacking attention with its crooked charm while being just a goofy, maritime impostor.

JACKHAMMER

The perfect tool for waking up your entire neighborhood early on a Saturday morning.

JACKPOT

The illusory treasure at the end of the rainbow, just a few billion losing lottery tickets away.

JACUZZI

Where you go to experience the thrill of feeling like a Hollywood star, without the inconvenience of actually being one.

JAGUAR

The animal that clearly attended fashion school in the jungle, always rocking the latest spots and stripes trend.

JAIL

Where you can finally catch up on all that reading, except the only book available is the phone book.

JALAPEÑO

The innocent-looking pepper that doubles as a fire-breathing dragon in your mouth.

JAR

A glass container that conspires with the refrigerator door to hide the one item you need until you've emptied the entire shelf.

JARGON

The secret language experts use to ensure job security by excluding everyone else from the conversation.

JAVELIN

The sport that combines the excitement of running in a straight line with the thrill of hoping your stick doesn't accidentally impale someone.

JAW

The body part that you never really appreciate until you have to hold a conversation with someone who loves to talk... endlessly.

JAW-DROPPING

The act of pretending to be amazed by something you've seen or heard countless times before, all for the sake of politeness.

JAYBIRD

A bird that insists on sharing your deepest secrets with the entire forest, because privacy is for the weak.

JAZZ

The art of making music sound like a crossword puzzle on a roller coaster.

JEALOUSY

The delightful emotion that fuels your passive-aggressive Facebook stalking skills.

JEANS

The versatile pants that can take you from "casual Friday" to "I forgot to do laundry."

JELL-O

The wobbly dessert that proves food should be both a solid and a liquid simultaneously.

JELLY BEAN

The candy version of Russian roulette, where one bite might taste like happiness, and the next, regret.

JELLYFISH

Mother Nature's way of reminding us that even the ocean has its share of spineless individuals.

JERK

The title bestowed upon anyone who forgets to use their turn signal while driving.

JEWELRY

Shiny objects that have the magical ability to make you forget you're wearing your entire month's rent on your fingers.

JIGSAW

The puzzle designed by a sadist, just to test your patience and sanity.

JINX

The magical power that compels your toast to land butter-side down every single time.

JITTERY

The sensation of consuming excessive caffeine and realizing you can now type a full sarcasm dictionary in 30 seconds.

JUJUTSU

The ancient martial art of attempting to untangle yourself from a human pretzel.

JOB

A daily adventure where you trade your time and skills for the privilege of funding your existence.

JOG

The art of moving your body at a pace that's slow enough to make a snail's race look thrilling.

JOHN

Because who needs an exciting, unique name when you can have something as plain as white bread?

JOINT

Where two bones meet to conspire against your comfort, usually when you least expect it.

JOKE

The art of making people laugh, followed by explaining why it was funny for five minutes.

JOKER

The card in the deck that reminds you life's a gamble, and you'll never have enough aces up your sleeve.

JOURNAL

The place where you document your life's adventures in exquisite detail, but only for about three days.

JOURNALIST

A person who writes about current events and is always on the hunt for the next typo in the newspaper.

JOURNEY

The "exhilarating" experience of navigating a grocery store on a Saturday morning.

JOY

The feeling you get when you finally find a parking spot at the mall, only to realize it's a mile away from the entrance. Better luck next time.

JOYSTICK

The device that proves navigating a spaceship or racing car in a game can be just as challenging as flying a real aircraft.

JUDGMENTAL

The endearing quality of forming opinions about others based solely on their choice of breakfast cereal.

JUDO

The martial art that teaches you to use your opponent's strength against them, or just to land softly when you trip.

JUGGLING

The performance art that turns otherwise coordinated people into public hazards with flying objects.

JUICE

The liquid that convinces you it's healthy because it once had contact with a fruit, but mostly tastes like sugar water with a hint of nostalgia for when you were a kid and thought it was actually good for you.

JUKEBOX

A relic from the past that lets you pay money to listen to songs you already own on your phone.

JUMP

The recommended response when you encounter a tiny bug on the floor, ensuring your bravery is known to all.

JUMPSUIT

A fashion statement that says, "I'm ready to take off into space or paint your house, whatever comes first."

JUNGLE

Mother Nature's way of saying, "Let's throw together a chaotic mishmash of plants and animals and see who can survive the humidity."

JUNIOR

A title that makes you feel important until you realize it just means you're the younger, less experienced version of someone else.

JUNK

Something you keep for years and then throw away one week before you need it.

JURY

The group of people who are clearly more qualified than you to decide your fate in court.

JUSTICE

A mythical concept often discussed but rarely witnessed in the wild.

JUSTIFY

The process of providing elaborate explanations for your actions, as if you're writing a persuasive essay for an audience of one: yourself.

JUVENILE

The age when you're simultaneously considered too young to do anything important and too old to be cute.

JUXTAPOSITION

The practice of putting a serene painting next to a modern art masterpiece, just to confuse gallery visitors.

Jail? Nah.
Stupidity is not a crime.
So you're free to go.

The letter "K"

K is the alphabet's quirky acrobat, performing high kicks and flips for attention. It's the show-off with a kangaroo's enthusiasm, thinking it's a karate master.
K stands for kooky kicks, kicking and cavorting around like it's a key player, but really it's just a comical, capering character.

KA-CHING

The delightful sound your wallet makes when it spontaneously bursts into flames from excessive spending.

KAFTAN

The oversized clothing choice for those times when you want to look like you're both fashionable and drowning in fabric.

KALE

The leafy green that makes you feel virtuous for a brief moment before you reach for the nearest bag of potato chips.

KALEIDOSCOPIC

The visual equivalent of having too many TV remote buttons to press.

KAMIKAZE

The ultimate example of a self-destructive hobby, as if skydiving weren't daring enough.

KANGAROO

A creature that combines the elegance of a deer with the posture of a T-Rex.

KARAOKE

The opportunity of embarrassing yourself in front of strangers while butchering your favorite songs.

KARAT

The unit of measurement that proves once and for all that gold is all about quantity, not quality.

KARMA

The cosmic system that ensures your good deeds go unnoticed and your bad deeds come back to haunt you with impeccable timing.

KAYAK

The vessel of choice for those moments when you want to paddle yourself into exhaustion and pray you don't tip over.

KEBAB

The excuse to eat meat and veggies on a stick and pretend it's a well-balanced meal.

KEEL

The ship's spine, because apparently, even vessels need chiropractic care.

KEEN

The word for people who can turn any casual conversation into a TED Talk.

KETCHUP

The preferred condiment for people who want their fries to taste like they're drowning in tomato-flavored sugar.

KEY

A tiny metal tool that transforms into an elusive ninja when you drop it.

KEYBOARD

The battlefield where you engage in epic typing wars and occasionally spill coffee to create modern art.

KEYCHAIN

A collection of colorful trinkets that somehow multiply and weigh down your pockets until they feel like anchors.

KHAKI

The color of choice for people who want to blend in by looking like a beige wall and for those who believe that fashion should be as exciting as a spreadsheet.

KHALIFA

A title that sounds impressive until you realize it just means "successor" or "caliph." Not quite as cool as it sounds.

KICKBOXING

The sport that combines kicking and boxing, in case you couldn't decide which body part to use.

KID

A tiny, unpredictable bundle of noise and chaos that occasionally resembles a human.

KIDNAPPER

The self-proclaimed travel agent for unexpected vacations.

KIDNEY

Your body's way of saying, "Two is better than one, especially when it comes to filtering out life's excesses."

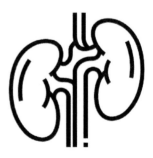

KILOBYTE

A unit of digital storage where a cat meme would max out your storage capacity in the good old days.

KILOGRAM

Because regular grams just aren't heavy enough to make you feel accomplished when carrying your groceries.

KILOWATT

The unit of power that makes you feel like you're single-handedly fueling a small village.

KINDERGARTEN

The artistic place where children discover that glue can be both a weapon and an artistic medium.

KINDNESS

A suspicious act of being nice, often leaving people wondering what your ulterior motive is.

KINETIC

A fancy word that makes movement seem much more sophisticated than it actually is.

KING

The person who gets to wear a shiny hat and sit on a fancy chair while everyone else does the actual work.

KINKY

The sophisticated art of making life's simple pleasures seem scandalous.

KIOSK

Where you can have a one-sided conversation with a machine and feel like you've made progress in human interaction.

KISS

The universal way to spread germs and awkwardness in one swift motion.

KIT

The perfect gift for someone you don't know very well but want to make it look like you put some thought into it.

KITCHEN

The room where you pretend to be a gourmet chef for special occasions, only to make cereal for dinner most nights.

KITE

A piece of paper and string that makes you believe you can challenge the laws of physics.

KITSCH

Because who needs good taste when you can have an explosion of questionable decor?

KITTY

A furry dictator who graciously allows you to serve its every whim, as long as you provide food and belly rubs.

KIWI

The fruit that always looks like it's having a bad hair day.

KNEEL

The humblest way to let your pants get acquainted with the ground.

KNIFE

The ultimate kitchen tool for asserting dominance over vegetables.

KNIGHT

A medieval cosplayer who takes dressing up way too seriously.

KNITTING

The hobby that simultaneously relaxes and frustrates you as you attempt to create a scarf that never ends.

KNOCKOUT

The perfect way to convince someone they need a nap, whether they agree or not.

KNOWLEDGE

The stuff you cram into your brain so you can impress people at parties, even though nobody asked for a lecture on medieval basket-weaving techniques.

KOALA

The cute fluffy animal that's literally a teddy bear but with claws.

KUDOS

The polite version of: "I have no idea what you just did, but good job!"

What goes around, comes around.

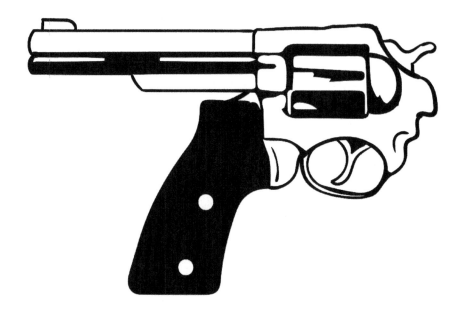

KARMA LOADING . . . .

|||||||||||||||||||||||||||||||||||||||||||||

The letter "L"

L is like a wonky chair, constantly leaning and struggling to stay upright. It's the alphabet's lopsided luminary, aspiring to stand tall but often taking a tumble. **L** stands for laughable leanings, pretending to be a leader while secretly being a lovable and lighthearted letter with a knack for leaning.

TINY JUDGMENTAL STICKERS

SOCIETY INSISTS

ON SLAPPING ON PEOPLE

LIKE PRICE TAGS

FORGETTING THAT HUMANS

ARENT CANNED GOODS.

LABEL

The quick and lazy way of simplifying complex individuals into bite-sized stereotypes.

LABORATORY

The place where scientists conduct groundbreaking experiments and spend hours trying to figure out why their equipment always malfunctions at the worst possible moment.

LABYRINTH

A maze so complex that even the Minotaur gets lost, proving that getting nowhere slowly can be strangely satisfying.

LADYBUG

A beetle that must be female, because who else would wear such a flamboyant red outfit and expect special treatment?

LAG

The cosmic force that delays your actions just long enough to ensure your defeat, usually blamed on "bad Wi-Fi."

LARGE

A word you use when you want to make your regular-sized coffee sound more impressive.

LAUGHTER

The best medicine unless you're at a funeral, a job interview, or a library.

LAUNDRY

The never-ending cycle of washing, drying, and folding that you secretly enjoy complaining about.

LAVENDER

The plant that makes your garden smell like a spa and your pillowcase a lullaby.

LAWN

A patch of nature you're forced to maintain, making you wish you'd rather have a desert landscape.

LAWYER

Someone you pay to argue on your behalf while you pretend to understand the legal jargon.

LAZY

A lifestyle choice that involves minimizing effort to the point where even gravity starts to envy your inertia.

LEAK

When your favorite water bottle decides it wants to share its contents with your backpack and important documents.

LEASE

A contract that allows you to temporarily own something, provided you make regular payments and never get too attached.

LEASH

A device invented to convince your pet that they are free to explore while secretly ensuring they never escape your watchful eye.

LEAVES

Nature's way of giving trees a colorful makeover and your yard an endless raking challenge.

LECTURE

An engaging monologue where someone talks at length about a topic you couldn't care less about, but they insist on enlightening you anyway.

LEECH

Mother Nature's bloodsucker, showing us that even in the animal kingdom, there are individuals who excel at financial exploitation.

LEFTOVERS

The food you refused to eat the first time, and now you get to avoid it twice.

LEGACY

The grand illusion that your existence will be remembered for generations, even though most people can't recall what they had for breakfast yesterday.

LEGGINGS

The pants that make you feel like you've made a fashion effort, even if you haven't.

LEGITIMATE

A word thrown around to add an air of credibility to something, even though it's often used to legitimize the most questionable of activities.

LEMONADE

The go-to remedy for when life gives you too many lemons, but you suspect that it's secretly plotting to throw limes at you next.

LESSON

A necessary evil in the journey of life, where you pay with your time and sanity to acquire a small nugget of knowledge.

LETTER

An ancient artifact that serves as a reminder of a time when people had the patience to wait for weeks to receive news from afar.

LETTUCE

The crispy, tasteless vehicle that holds your salad dressing hostage, making every bite a thrilling game of Russian Roulette.

LEVERAGE

The art of convincing someone to do your bidding while making them believe it was their idea all along. It's like mind control, but with plausible deniability.

LIBERTY

The delightful fantasy that you're free to do whatever you want, as long as you obey countless rules, laws, and societal expectations.

LIBRARY

A place where the faintest whisper can earn you a lifetime ban, and the librarian is the silent overlord you dare not cross.

LICENSE

A small piece of paper that magically transforms terrible drivers into legally terrible drivers.

LIE

The glue that holds society together, or so some politicians seem to believe.

LIFE

The universe's way of throwing random challenges at you just to see how well you can juggle.

LIGHT

The cosmic flashlight responsible for both brightening your day and reminding you of the dust on your furniture.

LIMIT

A word invented to keep overachievers from taking over the universe.

LINGERIE

The tiny, lacy pieces of fabric that remind you how impractical fashion can be.

LIPSTICK

A cosmetic product that promises to transform your lips but usually ends up coloring everything else your lips come into contact with.

LITERATURE

The art of writing impressive-sounding sentences about mundane things, like describing a sunset as "the ethereal descent of the solar orb."

LLAMA

Nature's most stylish neck warmer. If you ever need a pet that spits at you and judges your fashion choices, the llama has got you covered.

LOBSTER

The ocean's answer to fine dining, a creature so delicious that it had to evolve a tough shell and giant claws just to survive the onslaught of hungry humans

LOCK

A mechanism that gives you a false sense of security until you realize it can be picked by anyone with a bobby pin and some determination.

LOGIC

A rare and mysterious force that some people claim to possess, often in arguments.

LOOP

The endless circle that reminds you that no matter how fast you run on a hamster wheel, you're still just a hamster.

LOSER

Someone so skilled and consistent at life that they always finish second, giving others a head start in the race of life.

LOUSY

A word often used to describe things that are so bad they're not even worth a decent insult.

LOVE

A complicated chemical reaction that makes you do irrational things like sharing your fries.

LOYALTY

Blindly sticking with something or someone even when it's clear you're on a sinking ship. It's called commitment, folks.

LUCK

The mysterious force that lets some people win at everything while the rest of us just watch in amazement.

LULLABY

A song that's supposed to put you to sleep but actually makes you question your taste in music.

LURKING

The art of silently observing online conversations without participating, like a digital ninja who prefers to remain unseen.

LUSTRE

The irresistible quality that prompts you to invest in a high-gloss, premium smartphone, which conveniently shatters into a million pieces the first time it slips from your grasp.

The letter "M"

M is like a mischievous mountain range in the alphabet landscape, showing off its twin peaks. It's the alphabet's melodramatic mogul, pretending to be monumental when it's just a pair of rolling hills. **M** stands for mountainous mediocrity, making a big deal out of a modest hump.

MAGENTA

Like red wine spilled on your favorite white shirt — bold, attention-grabbing, and impossible to ignore.

MAGIC

The only job where sawing your assistant in half can lead to a standing ovation instead of a court summons.

MAGICIAN

The master of sleight-of-hand and illusions, who can make a rabbit disappear, and your wallet, too.

MAGNET

A tiny piece of metal that magically attracts all your spare change, paperclips, and hopes of a clutter-free desk.

MAKEUP

The magical art of enhancing your appearance, making you look like you've had eight hours of sleep when you've only had three.

MANICURE

A short-lived moment of nail perfection that's immediately ruined by everyday tasks like opening a soda can.

MANNER

A mysterious concept that seems to vanish when people step onto public transportation.

MAP

A schematic representation of an area you are completely lost in.

MARGARINE

The butter substitute that tastes nothing like butter but claims to be "heart-healthy."

MARKETING

The art of convincing you that you desperately need something you didn't even know existed.

MARRIAGE

The art of legally binding two people together, often accompanied by the ceremonial sacrifice of personal space.

MASCARA

The beauty product that promises to give your lashes the volume of a peacock but usually ends up looking like a clumpy spider.

MASK

The fashionable accessory that lets you breathe your own recycled air while convincing everyone you're a mysterious superhero.

MATH

A subject that makes you wonder why letters are hanging out with numbers.

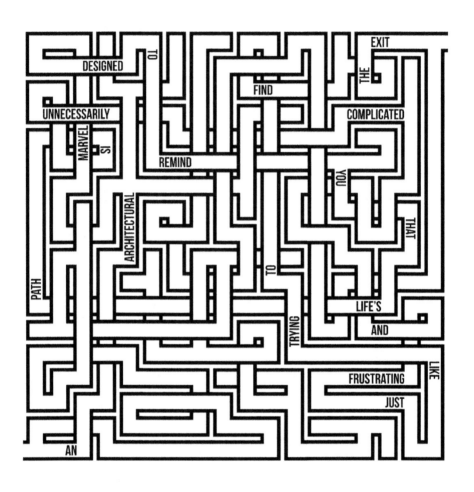

MEAT

The culinary delight that proves humans are at the top of the food chain, but sometimes at the expense of other species' peace and quiet.

MEDIA

Your daily dose of sensationalism, where minor events are reported as the apocalypse, and the apocalypse is just another headline.

MEDICINE

A remedy for ailments that, when taken as prescribed, usually comes with a list of side effects that sound worse than the original problem.

MEDITATION

A practice that involves sitting in silence and trying to clear your mind, all while thinking about everything you need to do after you finish meditating.

MEETINGS

A form of organized torture where people gather to discuss things they could have resolved in a single email.

MEMORY

The thing that fails you when you need it most but excels at reminding you of embarrassing moments.

MESSAGE

The modern-day equivalent of carrier pigeons, except with a much higher risk of autocorrect fails.

METEOROLOGY

The science of making predictions about the weather with the same accuracy as flipping a coin.

MICROPHONE

The auditory megaphone that amplifies your embarrassing background noises during virtual meetings.

MICROWAVE

A magic food-heating box that can turn your frozen food into lava in 10 seconds.

MILK

The drink that single-handedly convinces kids that cows are magical udder-fountains of deliciousness.

MIME

The perfect career choice for those who excel at explaining things to invisible friends.

MINIMALISM

The art of owning as little as possible, except for the expensive book that taught you how to do it.

MINUTE

A measurement that sounds insignificant until you realize you've been on hold for "just a minute" for the past half-hour.

MIRROR

The object that reminds you that your hair only looks good when no one is around.

MISCOMMUNICATION

The art of speaking the same language but somehow still managing to confuse everyone involved.

MITTENS

The impractical gloves that make you feel like you have sausage fingers while attempting to button your coat.

MMORPG

The massive online worlds where you can be a hero, forge alliances, or just spend hours customizing your character's hairstyle.

MOCKINGBIRD

The avian impersonator that turns your peaceful morning into an endless loop of car alarms and cell phone ringtones.

MOM

The ultimate multitasker who can cook, clean, work, and listen to your problems all at the same time while still asking if you've eaten.

MONDAY

The day of the week specially designed to test your patience and caffeine tolerance.

MONOPOLY

The capitalist fever dream that teaches you to buy up entire neighborhoods and destroy friendships in the process.

MOON

The celestial body that has witnessed more romantic clichés and werewolf transformations than any other.

MOP

A clever invention designed to spread dirty water around your floors, making you wonder if you're actually cleaning or just playing in a puddle.

MOSQUITO

Nature's reminder that even the smallest things can be incredibly annoying.

MOSS

Nature's lovely carpet, thriving in places you never knew existed.

MOTEL

The glamorous cousin of hotels, where you can enjoy a cozy night's stay with bonus surprises like mysterious stains and flickering neon signs.

MOTH

The butterfly's less glamorous cousin, inexplicably drawn to your wardrobe's finest fabrics.

MOUSE

The reason your desk has more tangled wires than a plate of spaghetti.

MUG

A drinking vessel that's always too hot to hold or too cold to enjoy your beverage properly.

MULTITASKING

The magical action of screwing up several things at once.

MUSEUM

A place where you can admire art, history, and the overwhelming desire to touch things that are explicitly labeled:

"DO NOT TOUCH."

MUSHROOM

A fungus that somehow divides the population into passionate lovers and fierce haters.

Mirrors can't talk.
Lucky for you, they can't laugh either.

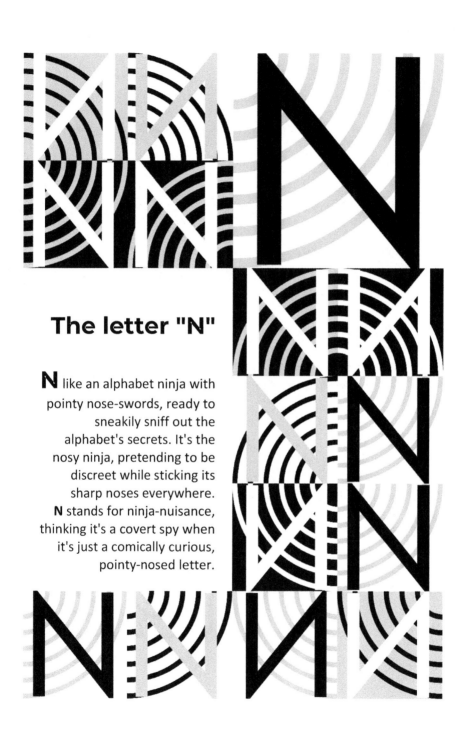

The letter "N"

N like an alphabet ninja with pointy nose-swords, ready to sneakily sniff out the alphabet's secrets. It's the nosy ninja, pretending to be discreet while sticking its sharp noses everywhere. **N** stands for ninja-nuisance, thinking it's a covert spy when it's just a comically curious, pointy-nosed letter.

NAGGING

The fine art of repeatedly telling someone the same thing until they lose their sanity.

NAKED

The ultimate fashion statement for those who believe that laundry day should be every day.

NAMETAG

The life-saving solution that covers the excruciating process of remembering names and solves any embarrassment.

NAP

A short sleep that leaves you feeling refreshed or confused, depending on whether you wake up five minutes or five hours later.

NAPKIN

A small piece of paper you'll use to wipe your mouth, only to later discover it's more effective as a coaster for your drink.

NARCISSISM

The art of taking so many selfies that even your mirror starts rolling its eyes.

NAUSEA

The ultimate diet plan – guaranteed to help you lose your appetite for everything.

NAUTICAL

A lifestyle choice that involves trading your car for a boat and your sanity for sea legs.

NEBULA

Space's attempt at abstract art, wanna-be Kandisky, showing off its impressive colors.

NECK

The body part that reveals your true age with the vulnerable stretch of skin, wishing you were an owl instead.

NECKLACE

A shiny, decorative piece of jewelry that conspires to tangle itself into an unrecognizable mess the moment you put it down.

NECKTIE

The noose of the corporate world, where style meets strangulation.

NECTAR

The elixir of the gods, unless you're a bee, then it's just your day job.

NECTARINE

A fruit that sounds fancy, but it's really just a peach pretending to be something else.

NEEDLE

A tiny, pointy instrument designed to play hide-and-seek in the haystacks of life, sometimes used for crucial sewing emergency.

NEGATIVE

The polar opposite of positive, the mindset that sees a glass half empty and wonders why there's even a glass there that can potentially be dropped and smashed.

NEGLECT

The automated process of turning your new to-do lists directly into the paper shredder.

NEIGHBOR

The free surveillance system your home has, working 24/7 and dodges your tall fences.

NEMESIS

Your unpaid life coach, someone you secretly admire for their ability to annoy you with such dedication.

NEPHEW

The little expert with a diploma in asking uncomfortable questions at family gatherings.

NERVE

The boldness to reply "k" to a paragraph-long message and somehow act like it's an acceptable response.

NEURON

The drama queen of the nervous system, always sending emergency alerts when it's just a minor inconvenience.

The human body has over 7 trillion nerves and some people manage to get on every single one of them.

NEVER

A word that suggest: "not now", "not today", "not tomorrow", "not next week", "not anytime soon", "not in this lifetime" and basically "not even in afterlife".

NEW

The term used to justify replacing perfectly functional things with slightly shinier and cooler versions.

NEWBORN

The most lousy and unique alarm clock you'll ever own. Best part, it doesn't come with a snooze button.

NEWSPAPER

The original clickbait, a relic of the past filled with yesterday's rumors, preserved for your coffee's table or doctor's office.

NICE

The most popular word used when people can't think of anything else to say about something that's just... ok.

NICKEL

A coin with a big personality and double-face, just like some people.
Worth five whole cents!

NIGHTCLUB

The human version of sardines in a can, where personal space doesn't exist and you enjoy being in the dark.

NIGHTMARE

A vivid dream that takes a dark turn, usually involving clowns, falling, or showing up to work naked.

NINJA

The warriors known for their exceptional skills in stealth, or for dressing up in black pajamas and pretending.

NIPPLE

The one body part that goes from innocent to scandalous with the mere removal of a shirt.

NITROGEN

The most exhilarating and essential part of the air you breathe, right after oxygen.

NO-BRAINER

An insult cleverly disguised as a compliment for someone's obvious lack of intellect.

NOCTURNAL

A term used to describe those who truly appreciate the art of sleep deprivation.

NONSENSE

The universal language people use when they claim that chocolate is a vegetable because it comes from cocoa beans.

NON-STOP

A term used by the shops open 24/7, except they are closed when you actually want to buy something past midnight.

NOOB

The affectionate term for players who are still learning the ropes, often accompanied by a gentle (or not-so-gentle) facepalm.

NOODLE SOUP

The perfect meal for those who believe soup should only contain one ingredient.

NOSE

The built-in sniffing device responsible for detecting the scent of freshly baked cookies or the unpleasant aroma of public transportation.

NOTEPAD

A revolutionary invention for people to write down brilliant ideas that will be forgotten as soon as they close the notepad.

NOTICE

A piece of paper that serves as proof that someone finally acknowledged your existence and that actions trully have consequences.

NOTIFICATION

A well-timed alert that conveniently arrives when you're actually trying to be productive... or take a nap.

NOWHERE

The ideal destination for those who are always on the run from their responsibilities, dreams, and adulting in general.

NUCLEAR

The technology that keeps us all in suspense, wondering if any world leaders are having a bad day.

NUMB

The exhilarating feeling you get after hours of mindlessly scrolling through social media, wondering where your life went.

NUMBAT

A marsupial that's always up for a game of hide-and-seek, as long as it involves... standing still in plain sight.

NUMBER

The magical concept we use to quantify everything, until we encounter letters in equations and the only result we get are headaches.

NURSE

The superhero wearing scrubs instead of capes, who also knows your entire medical history better than you do.

NUTRIENT

The stuff in vegetables that keeps you alive, tricking you into eating them, even if they taste like cardboard sometimes.

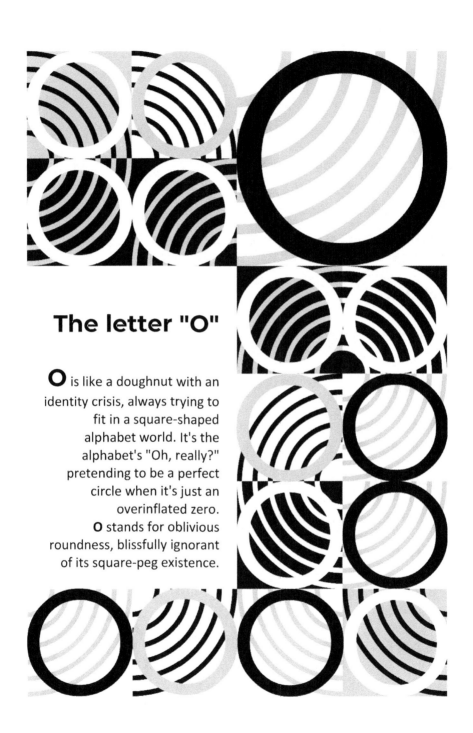

The letter "O"

O is like a doughnut with an identity crisis, always trying to fit in a square-shaped alphabet world. It's the alphabet's "Oh, really?" pretending to be a perfect circle when it's just an overinflated zero. **O** stands for oblivious roundness, blissfully ignorant of its square-peg existence.

OATMEAL

The breakfast that makes you feel like a responsible adult, even when you'd rather have pancakes.

OBESE

The condition where your favorite exercise is lifting a fork to your mouth.

OBEY

The brilliant strategy of letting someone else make all the questionable decisions.

OBSCURE

Something so unknown, even Google gives up trying to find information about it.

OBSTACLE

The magical object that appears when you're in a hurry and disappears when you have all the time in the world.

OCCASION

The rare moment when you contemplate leaving your comfort zone.

OCCULT

The belief in secret knowledge and magical rituals that usually involve a lot of candles.

OCEAN

The planet's gigantic bathtub, watery playground for all the things that want to eat you.

OCTAGON

The shape that makes circles and squares jealous of its uniqueness.

OCTOPUS

The friendliest creature that could slap eight people at once, in a heartbeat.

OFFEND

The accidental talent of turning innocent words into weapons.

OLIVE

The edible garnish that taunts you with its slippery nature while trying to escape your fork.

OMELETTE

The culinary masterpiece that lets you hide all your failed cooking attempts under a layer of eggs.

OMNIPRESENT

The quality of being everywhere at once, as long as "everywhere" means the couch and the fridge.

ONION

The vegetable that single-handedly keeps the tissue industry in business, adding flavor to your meals and tears to your eyes, reminding you that sometimes life's greatest joys come with a little pain.

ONLINE

The wonderland where you can Google your symptoms and convince yourself you're dying, one search at a time.

ON-TIME

The elusive concept that only exists in theory and airline advertisements.

OPACITY

The art of being as clear as mud in your communication.

OPEN-MINDED

The quality you claim to have when you're trying to win an argument.

OPINION

Something everyone has but only a few should share.

OPPONENT

The person who will become your best friend if they lose, but your sworn enemy if they win.

OPPORTUNIST

Someone who sees an open door and promptly slams it shut on others.

OPPOSITES

The concept that helps you realize you and your roommate have absolutely nothing in common.

OPTIMISM

The audacity to believe that traffic will be smooth during rush hour.

OPTIMIZATION

The belief that if something can be made better, then it absolutely should be, even if it's already working perfectly fine.

ORCHESTRA

A group of talented musicians who willingly follow the whims of a conductor with a stick.

ORCHID

A flower so fancy, it's basically the diva of the floral world, demanding attention and a VIP spot on your windowsill.

ORDINARY

The art of blending in so well that nobody notices you exist.

OREGANO

The ingredient that converts any chef into an expert in the culinary mysteries of Italy.

ORGANIC

A label on overpriced food that somehow makes it taste healthier and more expensive.

ORIGINALITY

The trait that ensures you're always one step ahead of the trend, just as it goes out of style.

OSCILLATION

The fancy term for something going back and forth, like your mood during rush hour traffic.

OSTRICH

A bird that reminds us that burying your head in the sand is a solid problem-solving strategy.

OTTER

The animal that's single-handedly keeping the "holding hands" trend alive.

OUTFIT

The clothing you meticulously plan, only to end up changing 17 times before leaving the house.

OUTRAGE

The sport of getting upset about things you'll forget in a week.

OUTSPOKEN

A quality people admire until it's directed at them.

OUTSTANDING

The polite way of saying you're so far ahead, everyone else is in a different galaxy.

OVEN

The appliance that convinces you to order takeout for the third time this week.

OVERBOOKED

The state of being so busy that even your calendar is begging for a break.

OVERCONFIDENT

The attitude you adopt right before life reminds you that you're not actually invincible.

OVERKILL

The level of dedication and effort you put into a task that really didn't need it, but you're an overachiever, so you can't help it.

OVERLAY

The digital Band-Aid that magically fixes everything wrong with your design, as long as you close your eyes and believe.

OVERTHINKING

The sport of creating problems that don't exist and solving them like a pro.

OVERTIME

The magical land where work hours turn into unpaid labor hours.

OWNER

The title you get when you pay the mortgage long enough for the bank to pretend you own your home.

OXFORD

The place where you can pay a fortune to learn ancient languages no one speaks anymore.

OYSTER

The shellfish (ocean boogers) that inspires people to spend an entire paycheck on a dozen tiny, slimy appetizers.

OZONE

The layer of the atmosphere that proves even Mother Nature believes in a good UV filter.

The letter "P"

P is like a pompous penguin in a tuxedo, waddling around with exaggerated elegance. It's the alphabet's posh parrot, puffing its chest out as if it's the ultimate in pomp. **P** stands for preposterous plumpness, parading like a portly peacock, when it's just a chubby, charming character.

PACKING

The intricate art of fitting way too many things into a suitcase and then wondering why it won't close.

PAIN

A gentle reminder from your body that you're still alive and, unfortunately, capable of feeling discomfort.

PAINT

The magical substance that turns even the most meticulously planned home improvement project into a colorful disaster.

PAINTER

A professional artist who managed to turn a childhood hobby into a career. They believe that "messy" is just another term for "abstract."

PAJAMAS

The outfit you secretly wish you could wear all day, every day.

PANCAKE

The ultimate proven method of testing the limits of non-stick cookware, in the name of fluffy breakfasts.

PANTS

The best way to dry your hands after washing them or scrub them when they're covered in flour.

PAPARAZZI

A group of highly trained photographers who dedicate their lives to capturing unflattering photos of celebrities so the world can see that even the rich and famous have bad hair days.

PARASITE

An uninvited guest that believes your body is a five-star hotel and refuses to check out.

PARENT

A sleep-deprived wizard who can summon magical bedtime stories on demand and has an uncanny ability to locate lost toys in the darkest corners of the house.

PARENTING

The exhausting job of convincing small humans that vegetables are not, in fact, tiny green monsters.

PASSPORT

Your golden ticket to experiencing the joy of airport security checks, customs inspections, and being treated like a potential international fugitive.

PASSWORD

A top-secret word that's so secure you have to write it down on a sticky note and attach it to your computer. Like abc123.

PASTA

The art of turning flour and water into an art of overcooking and undercooking.

PAYDAY

The magical day when your bank account experiences a brief moment of happiness before bills come crashing down like an avalanche.

PENCIL

A writing tool that always disappears when you need it most, only to reappear when you no longer need to write anything down.

PENGUIN

Bird who missed the memo about flying and decided to embrace the tuxedo-wearing, waddling lifestyle instead.

PENSION

A magical fund that promises to support you through your golden years, as long as you've mastered the art of living on a budget equivalent to a hamster's allowance.

PERFECT

An ideal state of being that's about as real as a unicorn riding a rainbow.

PERFUME

A mysterious concoction that turns you into a walking air freshener, ensuring everyone around you knows when you've arrived.

PESSIMIST

An optimist with real world experience.

PHOBOPHOBIA

Being afraid of being afraid, afraidception or something like that.

PIG

The animal that's the ultimate role model for those who believe that rolling in the dirt is a legitimate form of #self-care.

PIGEONS

The urban residents who majestically decorate statues with their artistic interpretations of modern splatter art.

PILLOW

A fluffy rectangle of comfort that offers blissful sleep and an unfortunate propensity to steal your earrings and hide them in the darkest recesses of its fluff.

PIÑATA

A colorful party decoration that brings joy to children and destruction to candy in equal measure.

PINEAPPLE

A tropical fruit that's the source of endless debate over whether it belongs on pizza or in cocktails.

PIRANHA

The world's most misunderstood fish, often portrayed as ruthless killers when they're just trying to enjoy a casual nibble.

PIZZA

A circular/triangle food that proves geometry can be delicious.

PLATYPUS

A creature with an identity crisis – part duck, part beaver, and all confusion, leaving scientists utterly baffled.

PLUMBER

A professional who charges you a small fortune to fix something they'll inevitably tell you was your fault.

POCKET

A mysterious portal where once-essential items like receipts and gum wrappers go to enjoy a lifetime of obscurity.

POEM

A delightful puzzle where the goal is to figure out what the author really meant when they wrote something that seems intentionally unclear.

POLICE

The diligent guardians of speed limits, always ready to remind you that you're not actually in a Fast and Furious movie.

POPCORN

A seemingly innocent snack that turns any movie night into a cacophony of crunching and an epic battle against the kernel that got stuck in your teeth.

POTATO

The overachiever of the vegetable world, determined to be part of every meal, whether you asked for it or not.

POTHOLE

A road feature designed to test the strength of your suspension and your ability to unleash a stream of creative expletives.

POTTER

A wizard with clay who can turn a shapeless lump into a beautiful vase and then promptly break it while trying to remove it from the wheel.

PRETZELS

Twisted snacks that inspire endless debates on the perfect level of saltiness, often resolved by consuming an entire bag.

PRINTER

A machine that holds your documents hostage until you've wasted half a forest's worth of paper and patience on ink cartridges.

PRIVACY

An outdated concept in the age of social media and surveillance cameras.

PROCRASTINATION

The art of avoiding responsibilities until the last possible moment, turning you into a productivity ninja under pressure.

PRODUCTIVITY

The illusion that you're getting a lot done when, in reality, you've just made your coffee in the afternoon after your long nap.

PROPOSAL

A well-planned big surprise where you ask someone to spend the rest of their life with you, just to see if they're really up for the challenge.

PSYCHIATRIST

The person you tell your deepest secrets to, only to wonder if they're writing a bestselling novel based on your life.

PUMPKIN

A versatile squash that serves as both a decoration and a flavor sensation during the fall season, only to disappear entirely on November 1st.

PURGATORY

The vacation destination for souls who were just a little too mischievous for heaven but not quite fun enough for hell.

PUZZLE

A frustrating pastime that consists of assembling hundreds of tiny pieces to form an image you could've just Googled.

PYROMANIAC

A misunderstood individual who simply has a deep appreciation for the aesthetic qualities of fire.

PYTHON

The ideal roommate, always up for a good snuggle, provided you don't mind sharing your bed with a 20-foot-long reptile.

There's someone for everyone
and the person for you is
a psychiatrist.

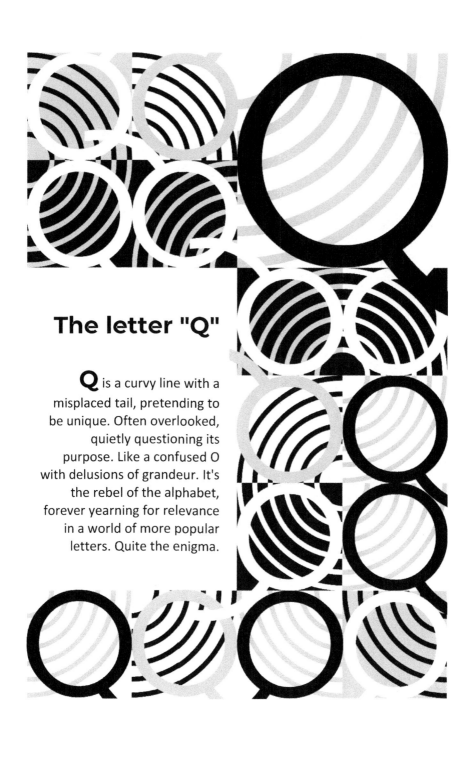

The letter "Q"

Q is a curvy line with a misplaced tail, pretending to be unique. Often overlooked, quietly questioning its purpose. Like a confused O with delusions of grandeur. It's the rebel of the alphabet, forever yearning for relevance in a world of more popular letters. Quite the enigma.

Q-TIP

The perfect tool for cleaning your ears when you want to defy all medical advice about sticking foreign objects into your head.

QUAD

A sophisticated way to say "four" for those who think numbers need fancier names.

QUADRANT

A way to divide a circle into four equal parts, because halves just weren't complex enough.

QUAFF

The sophisticated term for "chugging," used by people who want to make their alcoholism sound fancy.

QUAIL

The bird that decided flying was too mainstream, so it just flops around awkwardly instead.

QUALIFICATION

The document you pay for to validate all those things you learned on YouTube and free PDFs.

QUALITY

A term used by those who believe "good enough" is never quite good enough.

QUANTITY

The measure of success for shopaholics and hoarders everywhere around.

QUANTUM

A concept in physics that makes you feel smarter when you mention it at dinner parties, even though you barely understand it yourself.

QUARANTINE

A state-mandated vacation for your immune system.

QUARREL

A friendly discussion, usually involving raised voices and pointed fingers.

QUARRION

The parrot that gave up on pirate impressions because it realized there's no future in it, matey.

QUARRY

The ultimate resort for introverted rocks seeking solitude and isolation.

QUARTER

The perfect calculated amount of effort you're willing to put into a task when you're not feeling particularly motivated.

QUARTZ

The mineral that always insists on being the center of attention in any rock collection.

QUEEN

The ruler of a land where wearing a crown is the only requirement for leadership.

QUEST

An unnecessarily dramatic search for something you're not even sure you want.

QUESTION

The verbal equivalent of a speed bump in a conversation, designed to slow everyone down and derail the topic.

QUESTIONABLE

The polite way of saying something is so sketchy that even your grandma would raise an eyebrow.

QUESTIONNAIRE

A collection of infinite questions that make you wonder if anyone has ever actually read your responses.

QUICK

The time it takes for your enthusiasm to fade once you realize how much effort something requires.

QUICKSILVER

The substance that moves so fast, it forgot to stop and introduce itself properly, making even the most patient alchemists giving up and switching careers.

QUIET

A mythical state of blissful silence that parents dream of but never experience.

QUILT

The heavy, patchwork blanket you reluctantly put on your bed during winter because turning up the thermostat is too mainstream.

QUIP

The ideal comeback for when you want to be sarcastic without committing to a full sentence.

QUIT

The solution to all your problems, as long as you're a fan of creating new problems.

QUIVER

The involuntary muscle spasm you get when your friend hands you a live insect and says, "Don't be scared."

QUIZ

A brilliant educational tool for proving how little you remember from last week's lesson.

QUOLL

A cat that desperately wants to be a raccoon but just can't pull it off.

QUOTATION

The thing you add when you need to meet the word count requirement on your essay.

QUOTE

A convenient way to borrow someone else's words and take credit for their wisdom.

QUEUE

The modern marvel where people unite in quiet camaraderie, proving that patience is a virtue, and boredom is its reward.

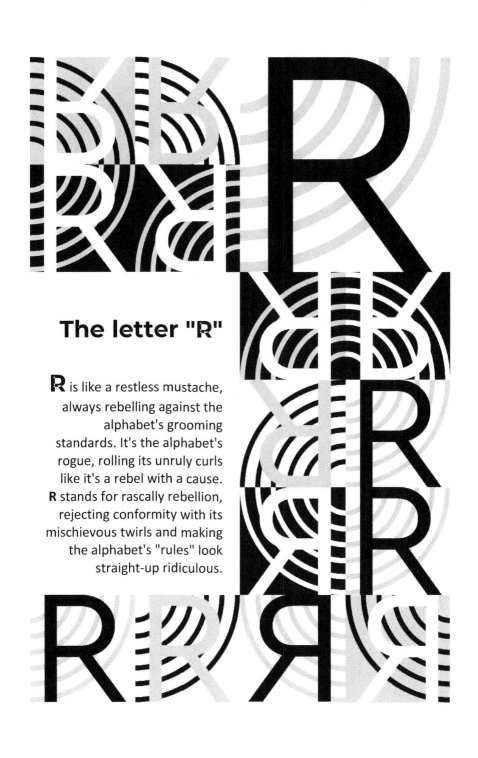

The letter "R"

R is like a restless mustache, always rebelling against the alphabet's grooming standards. It's the alphabet's rogue, rolling its unruly curls like it's a rebel with a cause. R stands for rascally rebellion, rejecting conformity with its mischievous twirls and making the alphabet's "rules" look straight-up ridiculous.

RACCOON

Nature's little bandit, always eager to redistribute
your trash.

RADIANT

What people call you when you've just spent an hour applying makeup
and filters for that "natural" selfie.

RAGEQUIT

The epic moment when your inner gamer Hulk smashes the controller
because a pixelated enemy outsmarted you.

RAIN

The ultimate hairstylist, specializing in the "drowned rat" look.

RAINBOW

The meteorological equivalent of a disco ball –
it adds a touch of sparkle to a cloudy day.

RAINCOAT

The only piece of clothing that manages to make you feel simultaneously
invincible and ridiculous.

RAMBLE

The fine art of saying a lot without actually saying anything at all.

RANDOM

The algorithm behind your social media feed that ensures you see the
most irrelevant posts first.

RANK

The level of expertise some people claim to have in a skill they've never actually tried.

RAT

The tiny rodent with a big talent for making you scream like a soprano.

RATIONAL

The act of using logic and reason, a rare skill in internet debates.

RAVE

An event that makes you wonder if you accidentally stumbled into an alien spaceship party.

READING

A hobby for those who enjoy staring at dead trees for the sake of intellectuality.

REALITY TV

The place where talentless people become famous for being talentless.

RECEIPTS

The tiny pieces of paper that seem to multiply in your wallet like rabbits.

RECYCLING

The guilt-free way to feel like you're saving the planet.

The Mundane Mart

Receipt

Customer : Adventure-Deprived Shopper
Date : Today, because who keeps track?
Cashier : Sarcastica Drollington

QTY	Item	Price	Total
2	'H2O Classic' Bottled Water	$3	$6
1	'Basic Bland' Sandwich Bread	$6	$6
2	'Adequate Air' Freshener	$4	$8
2	Generic Instant Coffee	$4	$8
2	'Regular-Flavor' Gum	$2	$4
2	'Zero Excitement' Canned Soup	$2	$4
1	'Non-Designer' Brand T-Shirt	$10	$10
3	Regular White Toilet Paper	$5	$15
2	'Unfashionably Neutral' Socks	$6	$12

	Subtotal	**$73**
	Tax 5%	**$3,65**
	Total	**$76,65**

**Thank you for gracing The Mundane Mart
with your presence.
We hope your next shopping venture is as
mind-numbingly ordinary as this one!**

REDEEM

The magical act of exchanging your hard-earned loyalty points for a coupon that expires before you can use it.

REFINE

The process of adding a pinch of sophistication to hide a mountain of mediocrity.

REFRESH

The deceptive button on your web browser that makes you believe it can magically fix slow internet.

REFRIGERATOR

The surprise ice wizardry box that turns leftovers into mysterious science experiments and requires a weekly archaeology expedition to find edible items.

REFUGE

The place you go to escape your problems, only to realize they've mastered teleportation.

REFUND

The process that takes longer than a cross-country road trip when you're in a hurry.

REGRET

A feeling that's always late to the party but stays long after everyone's gone.

REINDEER

Santa's underpaid, overworked, and criminally underappreciated transportation team.

RELAXATION

The fantasy of taking a break that's interrupted by someone saying, "Are you busy?"

RELIEF

The fleeting emotion you experience when your alarm goes off on Monday morning, and you realize its Saturday.

REMEDY

The magical cure-all that works about as well as wishing on a shooting star.

REMEMBER

The superpower you wish you had when you walk into a room and immediately forget why you went there.

RENDER

The digital wizardry that turns your computer into a space heater while it tries to complete a task.

REPAIR

The activity that turns a five-minute task into a week-long DIY project, even with the mastery of superglue and duct tape.

RESCUE

The heroic act of saving someone from a minor inconvenience, like holding a door open for them.

RESEARCH

The art of making Google think you're an expert on any topic in 10 minutes or less.

RESELL

The ingenious business strategy of convincing someone that their junk is actually your treasure.

RESOURCE

That thing you realize you should've read after you've already completed the project.

RESPAWN

The phoenix-like rebirth that lets you try again after being spectacularly obliterated by a boss.

REST

That elusive state of mind you chase all week but never catch.

RESTAURANT

The culinary arena where you discover your tolerance for spicy food and the limits of your wallet.

RESULT

The evidence that life has a twisted sense of humor, often laughing at your expectations.

RESURRECT

The act of trying to revive a long-abandoned New Year's resolution, even though January was, like, ten months ago.

REUNITE

The heartwarming event where you gather with old acquaintances to remember why you lost touch in the first place.

REVENGE

Once day you know you're gonna make onion cries.

REWARD

What you receive for completing a task you were already obligated to do, as if it were a generous gift.

RIBBON

The decorative strip of fabric that makes your gift look way more expensive than it actually is.

RISK

The rush of adrenaline that temporarily makes you forget your common sense.

ROBOT

Your future co-worker that never takes a break, never complains about the coffee, and never participates in office gossip.

ROCKSTAR

The occupation that seems awesome until you realize it involves more waiting backstage than actual rocking.

ROSE

The classic gift that says, "I couldn't think of anything else, so here's something that'll die in a week."

ROTTWEILER

A breed of dog that doubles as a security system and a cuddle partner.

RULER

The straightedge that can transform into a makeshift sword in the hands of a bored student.

RUM

The pirate's potion, because who needs treasure maps when you have a bottle of this?

The letter "S"

S is like a slippery snake in the alphabet's garden, hissing and slithering its way into words. It's the alphabet's sly trickster, showcasing its curvy moves like it's a superstar. **S** stands for serpentine showmanship, sashaying into sentences with style, but deep down, it's just a slippery character.

SACRIFICE

The noble act of giving up something you never really wanted in the first place, just to show off your selflessness.

SAFE

The reassuring box where you keep your most valuable possessions, conveniently labeled for burglars so they know exactly where to look.

SAFETY

The elusive concept of wrapping yourself in bubble wrap and hiding under your bed to avoid all possible risks, while still somehow managing to stub your toe.

SAINT

A person so holy that they can walk on water, turn water into wine, and still make you feel guilty for not recycling.

SALVAGE

The art of rescuing something from the brink of usefulness, just so you can remind yourself why it was discarded in the first place.

SANE

A condition that afflicts those unfortunate individuals who never experienced the thrill of talking to their toaster as if it were a therapist.

SANITARY

A term used to describe conditions that are slightly less horrifying than those in a horror movie, but only just.

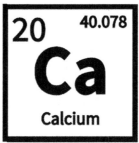

SARCASM

The true language of intellectuals, if you didn't already know.

SAUSAGE

Ground meat encased in its own intestines, somehow managing to taste delicious despite sounding vaguely disturbing.

SAVE

The noble endeavor of putting aside a small fraction of your paycheck each month, with the faint hope that you'll have enough to retire in 100 years.

SCISSORS

The only tool capable of defeating the indestructible packaging of your online purchases.

SCULPTOR

Someone who can turn a chunk of stone into something resembling a person and call it "art." Bonus points if it confuses pigeons.

SECURE

The illusion that your computer is impenetrable because you've chosen "password123" as your password, fooling hackers with your sheer audacity.

SENIOR

A walking encyclopedia of unsolicited life advice, ready to share their wisdom whether you asked for it or not.

SHINE

A quality possessed by some people's foreheads on hot and humid days, giving them an otherworldly glow.

SHOVEL

The most versatile tool in winter, used for digging out frozen cars, sculpting snowmen, and defending your kingdom, of course.

SHOWER

A slow process that consists of 5% washing, 20% singing and 75% winning fake arguments.

SHRIMP

The ocean's contribution to the world of appetizers, providing a whopping two bites of flavor per serving.

SIBLING

A special someone you'd give a kidney but wouldn't allow them to borrow your charger.

SKILL

The talent for turning simple tasks into unnecessarily complex endeavors, all in the name of impressing absolutely no one.

SLEEP

The daily practice of lying in bed, staring at the ceiling, and contemplating your life choices until you run out of regrets to count.

SLOTH

Nature's true Zen master, teaching us the art of extreme relaxation and how to take it easy, by doing absolutely nothing at all.

SMARTPHONE

A pocket-sized portal to the entire world that you use mainly to take pictures of your food and ignore incoming calls.

SNAIL

Nature's practical joke, reminding us that slow and steady might not win the race but will certainly test our patience.

SNOW

Nature's way of turning your morning commute into a real-life game of Mario Kart.

SNOWFLAKE

Each one unique, just like your attempts to catch them on your tongue.

SOCKS

Foot prisons designed to go missing in the laundry, leaving you with a collection of mismatched orphans.

SOFA

The ideal place to put laundry that you don't feel like folding, effectively turning it into a decorative piece of your living room.

SOFT

A term to describe someone who can't handle even the gentlest criticism, like a marshmallow in the face of constructive feedback.

SOUND

The amazing phenomenon where your child's laughter can fill your heart with joy or your home with chaos, depending on the volume and context.

SOUP

The culinary masterpiece that convinces you vegetables can be a main course, as long as they're floating in a sea of broth.

SPARKLES

The tiny, glittery particles that have an uncanny ability to defy the laws of physics by getting absolutely everywhere, no matter how careful you are.

SPEAKERS

The audio conduits responsible for broadcasting your questionable taste in music to the entire neighborhood.

SPEEDRUN

The art of completing a game in record time, requiring skill, precision, and unhealthy amounts of caffeine.

SPIDER

Nature's home security system, diligently weaving webs to catch trespassing insects and your misplaced keys.

SPINACH

The iron-rich green that promises to make you strong like Popeye but often ends up in a creamy dip.

SPOIL

The noble act of ensuring that your children never experience disappointment, adversity, or the concept of "earning."

SPONGE

The kitchen accessory that's always two weeks away from developing its own ecosystem.

SPRING

The season that tricks you into thinking you've finally made it through winter, only to surprise you with more weather mood swings.

STAGE

The place where actors go to dramatically pretend they're someone else, so you can pretend to care for a couple of hours.

STAIRS

A devious architectural feature that transforms everyday tasks into cardio workouts and reminds you that gravity is your nemesis.

STRESS

The body's way of reminding you that relaxation is for the weak.

SUCCULENT

The low-maintenance friend of the plant kingdom, thriving on neglect and sporadic waterings.

SUDOKU

The puzzle game that makes you feel like a math genius until you realize you've been stuck on the same square for 30 minutes.

SUMMER

The season that turns your car into an oven and your clothing into a game of "How little can I wear without getting arrested?"

SUNBURN

The seasonal souvenir that turns you into a walking lobster and makes you reevaluate your sunscreen strategy.

SUNGLASSES

Mysterious eyewear that allows you to discreetly stare at people without revealing your true intentions.

SWAN

The majestic bird that has perfected the art of making every other waterfowl look like a clumsy, feathered amateur.

SWEATPANTS

Fashion's way of saying, "I've surrendered to comfort, and I'm not ashamed."

SYNONYM

A word used in place of the one you can't spell.

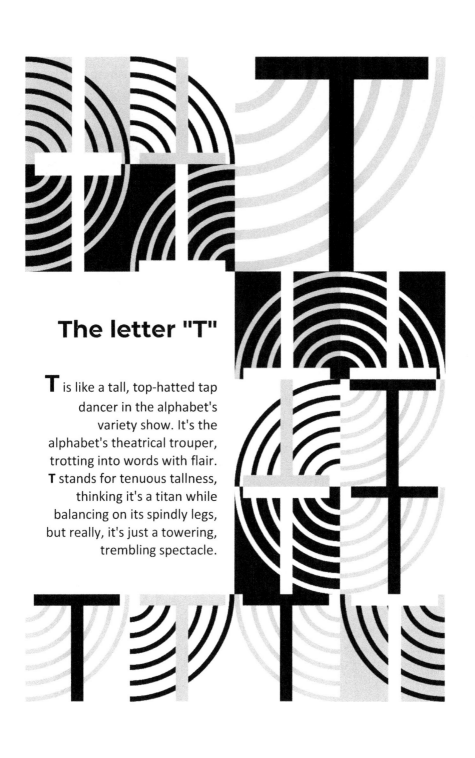

The letter "T"

T is like a tall, top-hatted tap dancer in the alphabet's variety show. It's the alphabet's theatrical trouper, trotting into words with flair. **T** stands for tenuous tallness, thinking it's a titan while balancing on its spindly legs, but really, it's just a towering, trembling spectacle.

TABLET

A device that's trying to convince you it can replace your laptop, but mostly just serves as a glorified e-reader and Netflix viewer.

TACOS

Portable flavor bombs that prove you can fit an entire culinary universe into a handheld shell.

TACT

A mysterious ability some people seem to lack when they speak their minds with brutal honesty.

TACTICIAN

Someone who excels at telling you what you did wrong after the fact.

TALENT

A rare and mystical gift that allows some people to excel effortlessly while others struggle just to tie their shoelaces.

TANGLE

The intricate dance that headphones perform in your pocket, ensuring they're inextricably knotted the moment you need them.

TARANTULA

The large, hairy spooky spider that's the star of countless Halloweens and horror films, despite being more fuzzy than fearsome.

TASTE

What happens when your culinary masterpiece looks nothing like the Pinterest photo but still manages to delight your taste testers... with sarcasm.

TAX

A mandatory contribution to society, which is then used to fund projects you'll never see the benefits of.

TEA

A warm hug in a cup, or as some might say, a leafy potion that requires elaborate ceremonies to brew.

TEACHER

A person who offers you problems and helps you solve them, sometimes.

TEAMWORK

The art of pretending to work together while secretly competing to see who can do the least.

TECHNOLOGY

The reason your grandparents still prefer handwritten letters and rotary phones.

TELEVISION

A device that convinces you to watch hours of commercials just to get to the occasional snippet of actual entertainment.

TEMPLE

A building designed to remind you that your lack of religious commitment is directly proportional to your inability to fold your hands properly during prayer.

TENDER

The process of meticulously preparing a meal, only to have it critiqued by your family with the enthusiasm of a Michelin-starred restaurant reviewer.

TENNIS

The sport that briefly turns you into a Wimbledon champion before you realize you have no idea how to serve.

TESTAMENT

A legal way to ensure that your family members have one last argument about who gets the old, rickety dining table.

THERAPIST

A paid listener who encourages you to spill your innermost thoughts and then charges you for the privilege.

THERMOMETER

A device that confirms you're feeling as miserable as you suspected when you're sick.

THIRSTY

The constant state of desperation experienced by your houseplants for a sip of water.

THOUGHT

A fragile entity that vanishes as quickly as it appears, like a soap bubble in the winds of distraction.

THOUGHTFUL

A word often used to describe people who occasionally remember your birthday.

THUNDERSTORM

Nature's drum solo, reminding you that even atmosphere can rock out.

TICKLE

Favorite form of torture from your siblings, that masquerades as a playful, friendly gesture, leaving you gasping for breath.

TIRE

A rubbery circle that mocks your attempts at having a smooth, pothole-free ride on the road of life.

TOAST

The miraculous transformation of bread from a squishy sponge to a rock-hard surface, often mistaken for an edible item.

TODDLER

A tiny dictator who rules your home with a combination of cuteness and temper tantrums.

TOLERANCE

The ability to endure other people's nonsense while suppressing the urge to roll your eyes.

TOMORROW

A mystical land where 99% of your motivation, productivity and achievement is stored.

TOOTHBRUSH

A stick with bristles designed to wage war against the plaque army that secretly invades your mouth every night.

TOPPING

The ingenious strategy of covering your salad with bacon bits and extra cheese to remind yourself that you're still living on the edge.

TORNADO

Nature's way of showing off its impressive twist and twirl moves where your belongings are now scattered across three counties!

TOUCHSCREEN

A magical glass panel that always seems to interpret your gestures as a random dance routine.

TOWEL

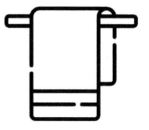

A fabric designed to dry you off after a shower and then mysteriously disappear.

TRADITION

Peer pressure from people who are no longer with us.

TRAIN

A vehicle that allows you to enjoy scenic views of industrial zones, graffiti-covered walls, and the occasional glimpse of a garbage dump, all from the comfort of your window seat.

TRANSLATION

The art of converting beautiful prose into a confusing jumble of words in another language.

TREE

The wise, silent observer of countless ill-advised attempts to climb its branches, inevitably ending in scraped knees and bruised egos.

TRENDY

A word used to describe cool fashion choices that will make you tragically uncool in a few years.

TRUSTWORTHY

A term generously applied to people who haven't been caught lying yet.

TRUTH

The one thing that everyone demands but is often disappointed by when they finally hear it.

**Trusting
people is like believing
that salt is just sugar's
rebellious alter ego.
Sweet on the surface,
but watch out for the
sodium sass!**

T-SHIRT

The unofficial uniform of adulthood, signaling to the world that you've given up on impressing anyone.

TULIPS

The flowers that stand tall and proud until they wilt and slump over, much like your motivation after New Year's resolutions.

TURN

The thrilling maneuver you perform in the grocery store when you suddenly decide that you need to revisit aisle 7 for the third time.

TUTOR

A person who gets paid to explain things you should already know but are too lazy to learn on your own.

TUXEDO

Formal attire that makes you look like a penguin impersonator, but fancier.

TWILIGHT

That magical time of day when you can't decide if it's too early for dinner or too late for lunch. Or that bad movie with vampires and werewolves.

TWIRL

A dance move that turns you into an elegant ballerina or a flailing tornado, depending on your coordination.

You never trully appreciate what you have until it's gone. Like toilet paper.

S. WHEELER.
TOILET PAPER ROLL.

No. 465,588.

Patented Dec. 22, 1891

Fig. 1.

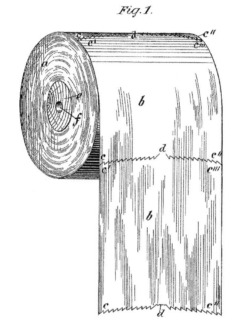

Fig. 2.

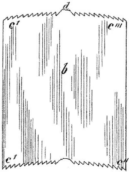

WITNESSES;
John Becker

INVENTOR,
Seth Wheeler.

The letter "U"

U is like a hammock in the alphabet's backyard, just hanging around without a care. It's the alphabet's laziest lounger.
U stands for unapologetic underachiever, embodying the motto *"Why work when you can just relax and enjoy the alphabet's scenery?"*

ULTRA

The label you give to your morning coffee when you add a double shot of espresso and whip cream, as if it's a health elixir and not a caffeine overdose.

UMBRELLA

A portable rain shield that takes every opportunity to flip inside out, revealing its rebellious side.

UNAFFECTED

The term you use to describe your reaction when someone forgets your birthday, even though you've been dropping hints for months.

UNBELIEVABLE

An adjective used to describe most of the stories your friend recounts from their weekend escapades.

UNBOX

The art of trying to open a tightly sealed plastic package without injuring yourself or launching the contents across the room.

UNCERTAIN

The state of being where you're absolutely positive about something, right up until the moment you're proven wrong.

UNDEFEATED

A term used by someone who's never lost a game of rock-paper-scissors, despite playing against themselves in the mirror.

UNDERESTIMATE

What you did to your opponent right before they crushed you in that game.

UNDERSTAND

What you claim to do when you're asked if you comprehend the user manual for that new gadget, even though you haven't opened it.

UNDERWATER

The exciting transformation of your garden into a waterpark after a heavy rainstorm, where your lawn mower doubles as a submarine.

UNDISPUTABLE

The label you give to your selfie as the greatest ever taken, even though it required 47 retakes and heavy filtering to reach perfection.

UNDO

The action you take when you accidentally like a post from three years ago while stalking someone's social media profile, hoping they won't notice your creepy digital footsteps.

UNEMPLOYMENT

The state of having plenty of free time to ponder life's mysteries, like why you can't find a job.

UNFAZED

The superhero power of remaining completely composed when someone tells you a story you've heard a thousand times before.

UNICORN

A mythical creature believed to exist in the same realm as common sense.

UNICYCLE

The one-wheel drive that allows you to demonstrate your exceptional balance skills while also ensuring that you're the main attraction at the circus.

UNIFORM

The dress code that tells the world you're a professional, but your choice of novelty socks tells a different story.

UNION

The organization that ensures everyone gets an equal share of misery at work, regardless of their actual performance.

UNITY

The dream of achieving global peace and cooperation, shattered every time you try to organize a group dinner and can't agree on a restaurant.

UNIVERSAL

The notion that all languages can be understood by simply speaking louder and slower, as if volume is the key to linguistic comprehension.

UNIVERSITY

The land of endless coffee, sleepless nights, and a degree that qualifies you for a job that may or may not exist.

UNICORNS
don't believe in humans.

They're just mythical creatures who pay bills and take selfies with brunch.

UNLIMITED

The marketing term used to describe your mobile data plan, which conveniently slows down to a crawl after using a small fraction of your data.

UNLOCK

The skill you master after years of practice, only to find that the key to success is hidden behind another locked door.

UNO

The card game where you smile politely as you slam down a Draw Four card on your best friend, secretly reveling in their misery.

UNPROFESSIONAL

The dedication to making your phone ring with the most obnoxious ringtone possible during meetings, just to keep things lively.

UNREACHABLE

The level of your ambition on Monday morning.

UNREAD

The status of 90% of the books on your bookshelf and 98% of your emails.

UNREAL

The quality you attribute to your ability to predict the ending of a movie, as if you've never seen a cliché plot twist before.

UNREASONABLE

Your boss's request for you to work overtime on your vacation.

UNRESPONSIVE

Your computer's way of telling you it's time for an emotional breakdown.

UNSTOPPABLE

The aura you exude when you manage to hit every red light during your morning commute, effectively setting a new world record for the slowest trip to work.

UNSUBSCRIBED

The feeling you get when you finally cut ties with junk email.

UNTOUCHABLE

The aura you emit when you're determined not to catch a cold during flu season, as if sheer willpower can repel viruses.

UP

The direction you're supposed to go in life, as if gravity isn't already doing its best to keep you grounded.

UPFRONT

The preferred approach for those who enjoy ruining surprise parties by revealing the surprise prematurely.

UPGRADE

The satisfaction of purchasing a "deluxe" burger at a fast-food restaurant, which essentially means they added an extra pickle.

UPHOLD

The noble act of defending a questionable tradition or decision like wearing socks with sandals, despite the judgmental looks from fashion-conscious friends.

URANIUM

The supposedly powerful element that's really just a rock until you figure out how to harness its energy for your DIY nuclear reactor project.

URANUS (THE PLANET)

The celestial body whose name still manages to elicit giggles from anyone over the age of five, proving that humor transcends space and time.

URBAN

The place where people go when they want to be surrounded by buildings instead of trees, traffic instead of tranquility, and sirens instead of crickets.

URGE

The overpowering desire to correct someone's grammar in the middle of a casual conversation, because clearly, syntax is the most pressing issue at hand.

URGENT

The urgency you feel to clean your entire house when unexpected guests are already at your doorstep.

URIAL

A type of wild sheep that spends its days climbing steep mountain slopes, just like you trying to reach the office coffee machine on a Monday.

USABLE

A generous way to describe that old, dusty treadmill in your basement that has served as a clothes hanger for the past decade.

USAGE

A term used to explain why you accidentally clicked "accept" on the 47-page terms and conditions agreement without reading a single word of it.

USER

The individual who magically develops amnesia about their own login credentials every time they need help navigating a website or app.

UTENSIL

The items you claim to use for cooking but are actually just for show, like that fancy whisk you display but have never actually whisked anything with.

UTILE

The rare and elusive quality possessed by that drawer in your kitchen that's somehow filled with utensils you didn't even know existed, let alone needed.

UTOPIA

The imaginary place where politicians always tell the truth, rush hour traffic doesn't exist, the person in front of you at the shop always orders quickly and efficiently, all your bills are paid on time, your laundry folds itself, diet consists solely of chocolate cake and ice cream and your vegetables magically turn into pizza in the oven.

1 universe
9 planets
204 countries
809 islands
7 seas
&

I had the opportunity to meet you.

The letter "V"

V struts like a voguish vampire in the alphabet's fashion show, sporting a sharp neckline. It's the alphabet's vain vixen, flaunting its fancy collar as if it's the trendsetter. **V** stands for vampyric vanity, vying for the spotlight with its sharp edge, but it's just a well-dressed villain.

VACANT

A term used to describe both empty houses and the expression on your face during boring meetings.

VACATION

A brief escape from the daily grind, where you spend most of your time arguing with your family in a different location.

VACCINE

A tiny shot of hope that that lets you experience mild discomfort now, so you can avoid a potentially major inconvenience later.

VACUUM

The magical device that gives you the delightful opportunity to rediscover long-lost treasures like paperclips, pennies, and that earring you thought was gone forever.

VAGABOND

A fancy way of saying "homeless wanderer" for those who prefer a more mysterious lifestyle.

VAIN

A state of being where one's self-love and admiration are so strong that it creates a gravitational pull, causing mirrors to spontaneously crack and selfies to multiply.

VALENTINE

The one day a year when you're reminded that your romantic relationship can be accurately measured by the size of the bouquet you receive.

Who needs a vacation when you can drink until you don't know where you actually are?

VALUE

The fictional number retailers assign to products before they decide how much to mark them down.

VAN

A vehicle designed for the sole purpose of advertising the driver's affinity for free candy distribution.

VANDALISM

The misunderstood art of expressing oneself through graffiti on someone else's property.

VANILLA

The flavor that people describe as "plain" when they don't want to admit they have no taste.

VANISH

The remarkable ability to disappear just when someone is about to ask you for a favor, leaving them pondering your uncanny talent for impeccable timing.

VAPOR

The enigmatic substance that fills up the room when you're cooking and triggers your smoke detector's curiosity about your culinary skills.

VASE

An ornamental dust collector that looks great on your shelf until you remember you have to clean it regularly, at which point it loses its charm.

VEGETABLE

The edible props on your plate, strategically placed to make the meal look more colorful and balanced than it actually is.

VEGETARIAN

Someone who eats plants to make cows jealous.

VELOCITY

The speed at which you make mistakes when you're in a hurry.

VENT

The modern-day megaphone for sharing your daily dose of first-world problems with the internet, with sound effects and melodramatic pauses included.

VENTURE

A risky expedition into the world of entrepreneurship, a way to burn money while convincing yourself that one day it'll magically turn into profit.

VENUE

The place where you can explore the true limits of your patience as you navigate through a crowd of people who are somehow always taller than you.

VERDICT

The grand finale of the courtroom drama, where all the suspense builds up to a momentous announcement that you could have guessed by flipping a coin.

VERIFICATION

The process where you prove that you're totally not a robot, even though you still struggle to fold fitted sheets.

VERITABLE

A fancy way of saying "absolutely, positively, and without a doubt," when you're not entirely convinced yourself.

VERSATILE

A word you use on your resume to convince employers that you can do everything, even though you struggle to boil water.

VET

The highly skilled professional who has mastered the art of deciphering the complex language of barks, meows, and disapproving glares from your pet.

VETO

The ultimate way for one individual to prove that their opinion is far more important than the collective will of the people.

VICTORY

The monumental accomplishment of finishing a crossword puzzle without resorting to Google or scribbling in increasingly illegible frustration.

VIDEO

The modern medium that allows you to effortlessly lose track of time, responsibilities, and personal hygiene, all in the name of staying "informed."

VIGILANTE

The self-appointed hero who thinks a mask, a cape and some questionable combat skills make up for a lack of legal authority

VILLAGE

The place filled with human surveillance cameras where "privacy" is just a myth.

VINTAGE

A charming way to justify paying extra for old stuff that would be considered junk if it weren't for a fancy label.

VINYL

The ancient relic people pretend to prefer over digital music, just to appear more "authentic" and keep their local record store in business.

VIOLET

The color that only exists in the crayon box, the color that's always second to purple but still insists on trying its best.

VIRUS

The microscopic troublemaker that makes sure you'll never underestimate the power of something you can't even see again.

VISA

A permission slip from your home country, granting you the right to experience the joys of jet lag and the challenge of navigating a new culture.

VISIBILITY

The enchanting quality that ensures you can always spot the public restroom signs from a mile away, but never the exit in a shopping mall.

VISIT

The biggest motivation someone can have to clean whole apartment in less than 1 hour, right before the visitors arrive.

VITAMIN

A substance you take in pill form when you can't be bothered to eat actual food.

VODKA

A clear liquid that helps you forget about your problems until the next day when they're twice as bad.

VOICE

A magical power that allows you to share your unsolicited advice on topics you have no expertise in, because who needs actual knowledge when you have confidence?

VOLATILE

A polite way of saying someone's personality is like a rollercoaster with no brakes.

VOLTMETER

The essential tool for those thrilling moments when you just have to confirm that your batteries are, in fact, dead.

VOLUMETRIC

A word that makes you sound like a scientific genius when you're really just talking about how much water your new water bottle can hold.

VOODOO

A pint-sized, pincushion therapist for those who excel at blaming inanimate objects for life's misfortunes.
Just remember, it's not you; it's the doll.

VORTEX

Nature's way of reminding you that it's the boss, effortlessly snatching away your umbrella and dignity on a windy day.

VOTING

The process of choosing the person who will disappoint you the least.

VOUCH

The noble gesture of putting your own reputation on the line to assure everyone that your friend's harebrained scheme is definitely a brilliant idea.

VOW

A heartfelt pledge to be there for each other through thick and thin, as long as neither of you gains more than five pounds.

VUVUZELA

A musical instrument designed to make you appreciate the sweet, soothing sounds of a car alarm.

If video games make you violent, does Monopoly make you a millionaire?

The letter "W"

W is like a double-visioned daredevil in the alphabet's circus, walking a tightrope with two "V"s for support. It's the alphabet's wobbly acrobat, waltzing through words with a split personality. **W** stands for wishy-washy wanderer, wobbling between its twin "V" personas.

WAITER

A highly skilled professional who magically disappears when you need more water or to bring the check.

WAITLIST

The exclusive club where you can pay money to get what you want... centuries later.

WALK

The chosen method of travel for those rare individuals who are allergic to public transportation, bicycles, and cars and would prefer experiencing the world in slow motion.

WALLET

A tiny black hole designed to devour your money, one transaction at a time.

WALLPAPER

The art of adhering paper to your walls with the expectation that it will never peel, bubble, or go out of style.

WARDROBE

A collection of clothes that somehow manages to shrink over time.

WAREHOUSE

The place where your online order mysteriously spends a week before shipping.

WARM-UP

The exercise equivalent of procrastination, because you're technically doing something but not really getting to the main event.

WARRANTY

A written promise that your new purchase will break just after it expires.

WASP

The insect with anger management issues, stinging you for the slightest perceived offense.

WATCHDOG

Your pet's way of reminding you that any potential intruder will be thoroughly licked to death.

WATER

The beverage that reminds you that you're thirsty right after you've already gotten comfortable in bed.

WATERMELON

A fruit that's 90% water and 10% excuse to eat an entire one in one sitting.

WATERPARK

The place where the terms "refreshing" and "exhausting" become interchangeable descriptions.

WAVE

The socially acceptable way to say hello from across the street, because nobody wants to risk close encounters anymore.

WEALTH

The ability to burn money for warmth during winter and enjoy it.

WEATHER

The only thing that can make you dress for summer and winter simultaneously and still be wrong.

WEBCAM

The digital eye that captures your best angles for Zoom meetings and ensures that you always look slightly more presentable than you do in person.

WEBINAR

An online "seminar" where you can mute yourself and multitask without anyone noticing.

WEDDING

A ceremony where you celebrate your love by throwing a party that's more about pleasing your parents than yourselves.

WEEKEND

The 48-hour period when you attempt to do everything you've been putting off all week.

WEIGHT

The reason why salads are invented but desserts still exist.

WHACK-A-MOLE

The game where fun means repeatedly smacking defenseless creatures that pop up and down like they're auditioning for a circus act.

WHINE

The universal language of toddlers and adults alike when things don't go their way.

WHIRLPOOL

A surprise spa treatment that occurs when you accidentally drop your phone in the bathtub.

WHISKER

A small, highly visible facial hair that somehow manages to grow at an alarming rate, usually right before an important event.

WHISKEY

The adult version of a security blanket, guaranteed to keep you warm and cozy on the inside.

WHISPER

A mysterious form of communication where people pretend others can't hear their gossip.

WHISTLEBLOWER

Someone with the uncanny ability to make powerful enemies just by telling the truth.

WHOPPER

A burger so large that you need a GPS to navigate its toppings and a nap afterward to recover from the adventure.

WILD

A term used to describe a party that ends by 10 p.m., with guests politely sipping herbal tea and discussing the weather... not.

WINDS

The invisible prankster that rearranges your outdoor furniture and messes with your hair.

WINE

The adult version of a juice box, because who needs a straw when you have a corkscrew?

WINGMAN

A friend who's supposed to help you pick up people at the bar but ends up stealing the show.

WINK

A skill reserved for people who want to look mischievous but usually end up just looking like they got something in their eye.

The winner
of the Astoundingly Average:
The 'Meh-dal' Recipient!

WINNER

A term often used by people who win an argument by shouting the loudest or TYPING IN ALL CAPS.

WINTER

The season that turns your driveway into a slip'n slide and your car into an ice sculpture.

WIRELESS

The technology that empowers you to search for your lost Bluetooth earbuds for longer than you actually used them.

WISDOM

The art of collecting life's bruises and scars while pretending they're medals of honor.

WISH

A magical spell you cast when you want something desperately, but you're too lazy to do anything about it.

WITCH

The perfect Halloween costume for when you want to simultaneously embrace and mock centuries of superstition.

WIZARD

An eXpErT who can miraculously fix your computer by turning it off and on again.

WONDERFUL

An enthusiastic way to describe something that's so average it's almost impressive.

WORK

An activity that people pretend to enjoy between weekends and vacations.

WORKAHOLIC

Someone who believes work is life's greatest gift and leisure is for the weak.

WORKDAY

A never-ending cycle of coffee breaks and staring at the clock interrupted by brief moments of productivity.

WORLD

A stage where you're expected to perform even when you haven't rehearsed, and the audience keeps changing the script.

WORSHIP

The solemn act of bowing down before your morning coffee, acknowledging its divine power to awaken you from the dead.

WUSS

A term reserved for people who have the audacity to express their emotions.

They say sleep is for the weak, no wonder I'm so f*cking tired.

The letter "X"

X is like an algebraic enigma in the alphabet's party, showing up uninvited and making everyone scratch their heads.
X stands for x-ray vision, peering through words while masquerading as a cross. It's the alphabet's undercover agent, keeping its true identity close to its chest.

XALAM

A musical instrument that only hipster musicians play, just to prove they liked it before it was cool. You probably never heard of it.

XANAX

A magical substance that turns your worries into unicorns, but only for a few hours.

XANTHAN

A modern marvel that allows you to create the illusion of culinary expertise by effortlessly thickening sauces and soups to a gloppy, unappetizing consistency.

XANTHINE

The secret ingredient in caffeinated beverages that makes you believe you're a superhero while you're actually just an over-caffeinated human trying to function.

XANTHISM

The belief that all fruits should aspire to be bananas when they grow up.

XANTHIUM

The plant world's equivalent of a passive-aggressive neighbor, whose seeds mysteriously find their way into your garden and refuse to leave.

XANTHOCOMIC

The sophisticated way of saying "yellowish" when you want to sound like you're discussing a rare and exotic hue instead of just plain old yellow.

XANTHOPHYLL

The botanical world's attempt at outshining the sun by adding a touch of dazzling yellow to every photosynthetic party.

XANTHYDROL

A mysterious elixir that promises to turn any dish into a Michelin-starred meal, as long as you don't mind a slight taste of gasoline.

X-AXIS

The secret code mathematicians use to confuse everyone else.

XBOX

A revolutionary piece of technology designed to make sure you never see the light of day, interact with real people, or accomplish anything meaningful in your life ever again.

XENOGENY

The revolutionary idea that plants can thrive in any environment, as long as that environment is a completely artificial, meticulously controlled laboratory.

XENOPS

A bird that proves evolution occasionally takes a coffee break and experiments with a beak design no one asked for.

XENOPUS

The frog equivalent of a Renaissance painting, featuring fully webbed feet, distinctive claws, and an air of amphibian aristocracy.

XEROX

The ancient practice of producing copies before the invention of copy-paste.

XIMENIA

A fruit that proves nature's commitment to variety by providing a taste experience that can only be described as "unforgettable" for all the wrong reasons.

X-RAY FISH

Nature's way of showing us that even fish can't escape the body image issues imposed by unrealistic beauty standards.

X-RAY

A magical device that allows you to see through solid objects, like your ex's intentions.

XYLOGRAPHS

The ancestors of pixelated images, reminding us of a simpler time when you had to manually carve every pixel with a chisel.

XYLOPHONE

The musical equivalent of giving a toddler a sledgehammer and telling them to play quietly.

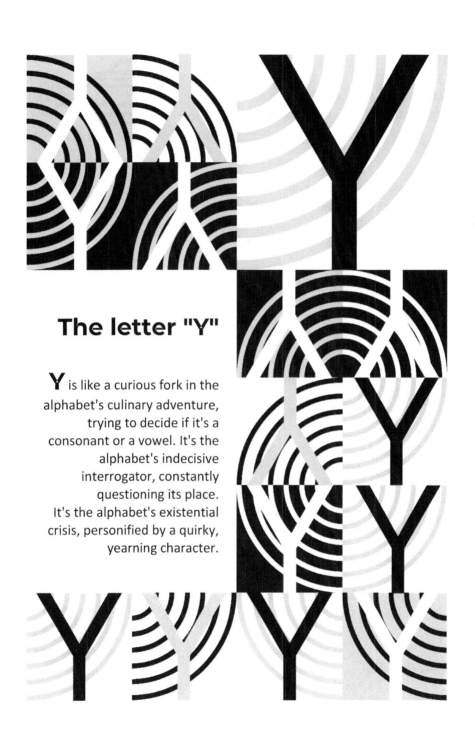

The letter "Y"

Y is like a curious fork in the alphabet's culinary adventure, trying to decide if it's a consonant or a vowel. It's the alphabet's indecisive interrogator, constantly questioning its place. It's the alphabet's existential crisis, personified by a quirky, yearning character.

YACHT

A totally practical and affordable mode of
transportation for everyday commutes.

YAK

A large, shaggy creature known for its impeccable fashion sense, often
spotted wearing the latest designer fur coats.

YARN

A magical thread that multiplies in your craft
drawer, ensuring you'll never run out of it,
especially when you need that one specific
color for your project.

YAWN

Nature's way of letting everyone know your boredom level has reached
critical mass.

YEAR

An annual opportunity for calendar manufacturers to stay in business by
selling the same 12 months over and over again.

YEARBOOK

A book filled with bad haircuts, awkward
smiles, and quotes you'll cringe at for the rest
of your life.

YEARNING

That intense desire for something you definitely don't need, like a seventh
pair of sneakers.

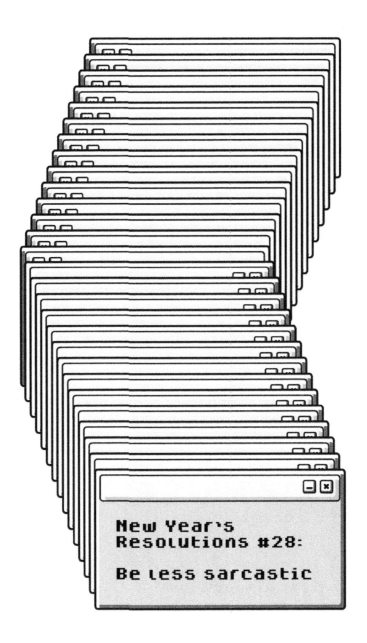

New Year's
Resolutions #28:

Be less sarcastic

YEAST

The magical ingredient that turns a bland lump of dough into...well, slightly less bland bread.

YELLING

The refined art of communicating so loudly that everyone in a 5-mile radius knows your business.

YELLOW

The color of caution, which is only heeded by those who can actually read signs.

YES

The universal response to a loaded question when you don't have the energy for an argument.

YESTERDAY

The day that seems to have a PhD in irony, always making you realize your mistakes just a little too late.

YODELING

The musical art form that brings joy to mountains and confusion to everyone else.

YOGA

A mystical practice where you contort your body into impossible positions to prove your superiority to non-yogis or your unimpressed cat.

YOLK

The golden reward inside an egg, just to remind you that chickens have been hiding treasures from us all along.

YOUNG

A time when you're convinced you know everything, only to later realize you didn't even know how to do taxes.

YOURSELF

The brilliant mind behind countless ingenious ideas that are promptly forgotten as soon as they're written on a napkin... Because sometimes we can't finish anyt-

YOUTH

The fleeting period of life where you think you know everything and can stay up past 10 PM without consequences.

YOYO

A small, round timeless device that reminds you of life's ups and downs, except with more strings attached.

YUCCA

The plant that's basically a desert warrior, thriving in arid conditions while making you feel guilty for overwatering your fern.

Is sarcasm a must?

The letter "Z"

Z is the alphabet's after-party crasher, always fashionably late and zigzagging its way into words. It's the alphabet's zany sleeper agent, snoozing through sentences. **Z** stands for zero urgency, zigzagging with the energy of a sedated sloth, a whimsical wanderer.

ZAG

The impeccable talent of making the most straightforward task seem like an intricate and complicated endeavor, keeping life endlessly intriguing.

ZARADOZI

The ancient art of meticulously sewing tiny, intricate designs onto fabric, typically practiced by those who have way too much free time on their hands and a love for squinting.

ZARANITE

The ultimate clickbait of the periodic table, promising untold riches and world-changing properties, but conveniently vanishing whenever anyone attempts to prove its existence.

ZAREBA

The word you pretend to know during a Scrabble game and hope nobody asks you to define afterward.

ZARF

The genius invention that caters exclusively to cups with self-esteem issues, providing them with their very own fashion statement to boost their confidence.

ZEALOT

A perfectly unbiased and open-minded individual who loves engaging in calm and rational debates.

ZEBRA

The master of disguise among animals, often mistaken for furniture or a well-placed throw rug.

ZENITH

The lowest point in one's life, typically marked by overwhelming success and contentment.

ZERO

The benchmark for success, an attainable goal that everyone effortlessly reaches.

ZIGZAG

A navigational technique so foolproof that it ensures you never reach your intended location.

ZINC

The element so precious that people often mistake it for gold and silver.

ZIP

The magical force that holds your pants together when you least expect it to malfunction, usually during an important meeting or a hot date.

ZIPPER

A small metal creature with a vendetta against fabric, whose sole mission is to chew up your favorite clothes.

ZODIAC

A celestial game that somehow determines your personality and life's direction. Because, you know, stars totally have it all figured out.

ZOMBIE

A fictional creature with a taste for brains, slow and lumbering movements, and an uncanny resemblance to the average office worker before their morning coffee.

ZOO

The animal kingdom's version of a reality TV show, complete with a captive audience.

ZOOM

A function so advanced on your photo camera that it lets you photograph a speck of dust on the moon from the comfort of your backyard.

ZUCCHINI

A veggie that has never caused any mealtime debates or picky eaters.

ZUCHON

A breed of dog so scary and intimidating that it can strike fear and nightmares into the hearts of stuffed animals.

ZUMBA

The go-to workout for those who want to minimize their heart rate.

ZYGOTE

A fully independent organism capable of fending for itself in the wild from the moment of conception.

Zombies eat brains. Don't worry, I'm pretty sure you're safe and sound.

Q sarcasm is   ✕ 🎤 Q

Q **sarcasm is** great

Q **sarcasm is** awesome

Q **sarcasm is** how i hug

Q **sarcasm is** a sign of intelligence

Q **sarcasm is** the use of irony to mock

Q **sarcasm is** a great way to start the day

Q **sarcasm is** the brain's defense against stupid

Farewell!

Now you're ready to tackle the world armed with the unparalleled ability to offend everyone while pretending it's just "sarcasm".

Printed in Great Britain
by Amazon

43180676R00142